Unleash
Your Full
Potential

**How to Start
Small and Build
an Empire**

Unleash
Your Full
Potential

How to Start
Small and Build
an Empire

George Wachiuri

CEO of Kenya's top SMEs 2014/15

Foreword by Bishop Phillips Katutu

Published by Sahel Publishing Association
P.O. Box 18007-00100
Nairobi, Kenya
Tel: +011-254-715-596-106
www.sahelpublishing.net

A Sahel Book

Interior and cover designed by Hellen Wahonya Okello
Editor: Sam Okello
Printed in India

To my dear and loving wife Mary Wacuka Kariuki and my children Jael Nyawira, Alex Wangai and David Wachiuri; my friend and brother Charles Muraguri; Honorable Nemesius Warugongo; my dear aunt Edith Nyaguthie Kimama; and the wonderful Optiven Ltd staff.

Contents

Acknowledgements

I give all glory to the Almighty God who has given me life, a great family, wealth, wonderful Optiven Ltd Staff and made our country Kenya peaceful and prosperous. I will always be a servant to serve Him, His people, our staff and esteemed customers. It is God who has given me the grace to make wealth (Deuteronomy 8:18).

To my caring, understanding, intelligent, intuitive and loving wife, Mary Wacuka, God is truly a matchmaker because Mary was carved for me and she has made me the way I am. Mary, I will always honor and cherish you in all my dreams. You mean a lot in my life.

To my wonderful sons David Wachiuri and Alex Wangai; my flower, the beautiful and awesome Jael Nyawira. The three of you drive my energy to do more; you motivate me and your smiles brighten my heart to keep serving the community.

To my mother, the great woman of Kieni, I respect you and you are special among all women on earth. You are the best God ever created. I value you greatly and you are my role model. I have learnt a lot of lessons from you: giving back to community, patience, honesty and revering God.

To my brothers Charles, Simon, JB Giticha, Francis and my only Sister Phyllis, I value you.

To all my dear and wonderful staff, you made Optiven be the best Overall Company 2014/15 and Best Company in Real Estate and Construction 2014/15.

To my Bishop Phillips Katutu and his wife Jacinta Katutu, from the day I joined Breakthrough International Church (BIC) in 2001, God has used you to encourage me; your teachings on empowerment have made me have a billionaire mindset on whatever I do. May

God grant you and your family many days to transform many more lives.

To my publisher Hellen Okello and Hon. Sam Okello, you have become very close family friends. Our association with you brings fresh air and you are such a model couple. You are a great resource to this nation of Kenya.

To Dorothy Kweyu, you took time to edit this book. I value you; you are extremely thorough in your work. Keep the talent going and share it with others.

To corporations that have given Optiven Ltd loan facilities toward our massive company expansion: Equity Bank, African Bank Corporation, Commercial Bank of Africa, Cooperative Bank and Kenya Commercial Bank.

To my mentors Dr. Wale Akinyemi, Dr. James Mwangi, Vimal Shah, Dr. Manu Chandaria and Hon. Uhuru Kenyatta, I watch what you do and you give me great energy that can uproot a "Mugumo" tree.

To my fellow church elders, Mr. and Mrs. Mark Wandungi, Wilson Mbugua, Loise Mbugua, Dr. Lucy and Geoffrey Kiganane, thank you for being an encouragement to me.

To our great authors James Karundu, Anthony Gitonga, Stephen Kigwa, Mbugua Mumbai, Sam Kariuki and Kariuki Kamau (KK).

Last and not least, my service providers: Wakini Kiarie Advocates, Prisca Maseno Advocates, Karingu Advocates, Lily Musinga Advocates, Kibanya Kamau Advocates, Czam Tax consultants, Value Max Auditors and Daveline Auditors.

To you, readers of this book, may you be inspired by this book in ways that your life, business and family will move to the next level of growth. It is possible and doable. Trust in God!

Foreword

Reading George Wachiuri's book *Unleash Your Full Potential* reminds me of one of the most fascinating books I have ever read. The book *It is Easier to Succeed than to Fail* was written by Dr. Truet Cathy, one of the most successful Christian businessmen in the fast-food industry, in America.

I was with George at the Gala Night event, where Optiven Ltd was declared the top among the Small and Medium-Sized Companies in Kenya—the year 2014/5. As the crowd watched George receive one of the most coveted business awards, I imagined what may have been going through the mind of those watching the glamorous event on their TV sets at home. *George must be lucky to have clinched this coveted award.* The imagination was that the award was like a lottery where the luckiest carried the day.

Having walked closely with George for more than a decade as a brother-in-Christ and his close confidant, I want to surprise you that this imagination is far from reality. George's personal life is punctuated with an ethos of life that makes him who he is and what drives and creates space for him at the top. He is a hardworking man, driven by unquenchable passion for success in everything he does. He wakes up by 4:00 a.m. I compare his ability to focus to that of an eagle that has spotted its prey from miles away and dives at a supersonic speed to seize it.

His dedication to God since he was young is admirable. More than once, he has called me to pray and dedicate his property before he begins to sell. He understands the value of divine help and can go out of his way to fulfill this noble conviction. I have heard him admonish his staff to give accurate distance to the property on sale and say the truth about the level of value already added to it.

Unleash Your Full Potential is a must-read for anyone who believes he or she possesses greatness inside but has been stuck in obscurity. He breaks it into digestible bits that even the simplest of minds in matters of business finds easy to grasp.

He shares, from his wealth of knowledge, nuggets of wisdom and the pitfalls to avoid at any level of business development. He doesn't hide from the reader his own failures so that we won't fall into the fallacy of thinking he has been all smart and gotten everything right. He so clearly walks you through how to build networks with people even outside your industry. George says it as it is—that "Network is Net worth."

I would like to thank George for this noble contribution to our generation and society at large. It has been argued that when it comes to entrepreneurship among the nations around us, Kenya is comparable to none. Although I am convinced that this book will be read and it will impact people across the globe, I am more persuaded that my fellow Kenyans will be glad you have provided practical solutions to the multiple problems they have encountered in their business start-ups.

My prayer is that God will inspire every reader of this brilliant book to aspire to start the long journey to success. Each of us can live our dream, like George is today, and see that dream blossom like Optiven Ltd has.

I wish to echo the tagline of this book: "Start Small and Build an Empire." That is the message of this piece.

See you at the top very soon!

Bishop Phillips Katutu
Breakthrough International Church

List of Tables

List of Figures

List of Abbreviations

A/C	Accountant
ASM	Assistant Sales Manager
BA	Branch Accountant
BGDM	Business Growth Development Manager
CBD	Central Business District
CBM	Corporate Brand Manager
CC	Customer Clerk
CEO	Chief Executive Officer
CCM	Customer Care Manager
CCO	Customer Care Officer
EAC	East African Community
EBS	Elder of the Burning Spear
ECOWAS	Economic Community of West African States
GE	General Electric
GOK	Government of Kenya
HCE	Head of Customer Experience

HRO	Human Resource Officer
IGAD	Inter-governmental Authority on Development
IMF	International Monetary Fund
KTN	Kenya Television Network
NTV	Nation Television
PM	Project Manager
PR/B	Public Relations/Branding
RA	Regional Accountant
RC	Relationship Clerk
RI	Relationship Interns
SA	Senior Accountant
SMA	Social Media Assistant
SME	Sales and Marketing Executive
SMC	Social Media Coordinator
SM	Sales Manager
SMM	Social Media Manager
SMO	Sales and Marketing Officer

SRC	Senior Relationship Clerk
SRO	Senior Relationship Officer
SSMM	Senior Social Media Manager
SSMO	Senior Sales Marketing Officer
SWOT	Strengths, Weaknesses, Opportunities and Threats
VAT	Value Added Tax

Glossary

Activity A situation in which something is happening or a lot of things are being done.

Amazon The world's largest online shop.

Boda Boda The use of motorbikes for public transport.

Break ice The ability and skill to open a conversation with a stranger.

Budgets Making financial plans and matching them with available or expected earnings.

Business Card A card with one's business information.

Buz environment Business environment.

Cash Flow The rate of inflow and outflow of cash into a business system.

Capital The required funding for a start-up business.

Copying Doing something in the exact similar manner someone else does it.

Core Values The values ingrained in a business system that guide its internal and external environment.

Corporate Governance All systems brought together to effectively manage a corporation.

Credibility Integrity.

Culture A way of life.

Customer-centric Focused fully on the customer.

Designs Things made to work a certain way.

Enthusiasm Vigor, joyfulness, gusto.

Events Occurrence of activities on planned dates and periods.

Executive Secretary Official responsible for record-keeping in an organization.

Exercise A given work to be accomplished for the greater good.

Expertise A set of skills required to accomplish a task with professionalism.

Facebook A social media platform popularized in the early twenty first century.

Fascination To be mesmerized.

Financial Controller Official responsible for finances in an organization.

Firing Terminating the services of an employee.

Focus Keeping one's eye on the ball.

Funding Availing capital for a business venture or any other kind of economic activity.

Giving Back to Community Using part of the earnings of a company to enrich the life of the community.

Global Conglomerate A business whose operations are worldwide in scope.

Governance Management.

Hiring Accepting the services of an employee for an agreed upon remuneration.

Homeostasis A state of calm or equilibrium.

Impact of Vision The way a vision affects those it was intended to touch their lives.

Implementation The act of channeling all energies toward actualizing agreed upon plans in an organization.

Inclination The overall bearing of a person.

Innovation The act of thinking outside the box to find new solutions and approaches.

Integrity Credibility.

Joblessness Being without a job.

Leadership Taking the lead in offering solutions and charting the way.

Location The geographical placement of an organization.

Mama Mboga A vegetable vendor.

Manager Official tasked to implement policies and oversees the smooth running of an organization.

Marketing Creating awareness about a given product.

Meditate Finding time to think about matters of life in the quietness of solitude.

Mentorship Being hitched to a person of given skills who holds the hand of one who lacks that set of skills.

Mission Statement A statement expressing the direction an organization desires to go and what it intends to achieve.

Motivation Being energized to get out and get work done.

Multinational Organization An organization with business across borders.

National Organization An organization with a presence only within one nation.

Networking Going out to meet new people who may later become business partners, clients, etc.

Nyoyo Boiled maize and beans.

Online Shopping Buying on the net e.g. Amazon.com.

Organogram A chart showing the levels of hierarchy in an organization.

Original Unaltered.

Passion Deep love for something or someone.

Policies A set of guidelines for an organization.

Prayer The act of worshiping.

Projections Judging behavior of the future based on the past.

Public Relations Ensuring that an organization is at peace with its external environment.

Requisite Skills Basic skill needed to accomplish a task.

Retailer A seller.

Role Model A person one admires and aspires to be like.

Small and Medium-sized Enterprises (SMEs) Enterprises that are not too small and not too large.

Social Media New forms of media like Facebook, Twitter, Instagram etc.

Socio-economic Perspective Viewing something from the social and economic angle.

Socio-political and Economic Problems Problems of a social, economic and political nature.

Strategic Planning Formulation Mapping out a blueprint.

SWOT Analysis Evaluating an organization based on its strengths, weaknesses, opportunities and threats.

Systems Structures that brought together form a whole.

Team Building Activities designed to create cohesiveness in an organization.

Teamwork Togetherness in task accomplishing.

To-do-List A list of activities and time they are to be accomplished on a given timeframe.

Twitter A social media platform.

Uji porridge.

1 Introduction

Ever since Optiven Ltd, the real estate company my wife and I founded, was voted number one among Small and Medium-sized Enterprises (SMEs) in Kenya, I have fielded many questions and been invited to give talks at our universities and in other companies on how to drive a business to the top. The experience of mingling with university students, Kenyans in the corporate sector and even leaders in politics has been as exhilarating as it has been rejuvenating. The trophies sitting in our head office are testament to the fact that we owe it to Kenyans and Africans to say what has worked and what hasn't so that our experience might be replicated tenfold across Africa for the betterment of our people.

Over the last couple of years our nation—and Africa in general—has gone through critical changes that have dramatically improved the business environment on the continent. This is not to say that such changes have not had unintended negative consequences as well; it is only to affirm the fact that a better business environment has emerged and should be taken advantage of by each of us. What follows, therefore, is for us to ask what role we should play, as business leaders in Kenya and Africa, to expand the space for business and create even greater opportunities for those who wish to get into business. Is there something we can do in Kenya, Nigeria or South Africa to brighten the future further?

I believe there is and that's why I have written this book. The unemployment situation in Kenya, much like it is across Africa, is at alarming levels; and there seems to have developed an attitude among our graduates that after obtaining a degree, seeking a job is the next logical step. I don't fault them for thinking that way because it is a tradition that caught on, but I also wish to underscore the fact that times have changed and new approaches to matters of making money must be entertained so that joblessness is reduced and eventually eradicated.

Most books written today on the subject of corporate governance and related subjects have been written from a typically Western perspective and though there are lessons to be gleaned from them, they lack a historical and socio-economic perspective upon which Africans

Unleash Your Full Potential

could anchor some of the findings in their studies. This book is written from a purely African perspective and will draw in many examples from this continent—with emphasis on Kenya. The observations, methodologies and teachings in it are drawn from lessons learnt right here in Africa. Does that mean we won't bring up examples from the West or the East? Far from it. We have to look at what has worked elsewhere and what has failed so that we have a solid base upon which to establish our recommendations.

What is Business

It is a conventional pattern to define terms using a dictionary, thesaurus or a book written by an authority on a subject matter, but many times I find some of those definitions grossly limiting or wholly inadequate in contextualizing matters—especially where Africa is concerned. For example, does the word business mean the same thing to *Mama Mboga* (vegetable vendor) as it means to a McDonalds franchise owner? Does the term SME mean the same thing to a Shanghai or Hong Kong mid-level enterprise owner as it means to a Nairobi or Lusaka one? Or does the term conglomerate mean the same thing to Bill Gates as it would to Kenyan billionaire Chris Kirubi or Nigerian tycoon Aliko Dangote? It is for this reason that I shy away from the use of standardized definitions and formulate practical, tested ones that answer to our peculiarities and sensibilities as

a people. But this should, in no way, be seen as a repudiation of Western business values, not at all. In fact, we have borrowed heavily from the studies and experiments of our brothers and sisters in the West and elsewhere; it is only in those *forgotten* areas where their experience has not been ours that we craft definitions that fit in with our circumstances and aspirations.

Business, in our context, is therefore *any* activity one engages in to make money. What Mama Mboga does is as much a business as what my mentor Vimal Shah does—the only difference is that Mama Mboga's is a small operation while Vimal's is a complex, large operation. This definition is deliberately simplistic to accomplish three definitional goals:

a. **It is designed** to encourage any of us to see business as a venture each of us can engage in and not wait to be employed (some people wade so long in the realm of job-hunting until they become professional job-hunters).

b. **It is designed** to make us understand that work is work. In Kenya, I have read stories in our newspapers, where graduates have resorted to roasting maize (corn) by the roadside to make money. Recently, there was a story of a graduate who has gone into the *boda boda* industry and now owns a motorbike to transport people for a living. The money drawn from these small businesses may be small, but it is better than nothing—certainly better than hunting for that elusive job for seven years.

c. **It is designed** to dispel the fallacy that to start a business one has to have huge capital and be prepared to borrow heavily from a bank. This is one of the reasons many graduates, and others with a desire to get into business, have felt discouraged and given up hope of ever owning a business. The truth is that you don't need a big loan to get going; you can get started, build your business into a thriving one, then seek those loans for expansion.

Recently, when I talked to young Kenyans at an event, one asked how long it would take to get to the point I am today if they started small like I was urging them to. The lady had a valid concern. In my case, it took years of pain, sweat, discouragement, failure, self-doubt and other unpleasant experiences. There was a day I even went to the office wearing different socks and discovered when it was too late to do anything about it. The day before I had lost the only money my wife and I had ever saved when I got into a sour deal. Sitting in the office that morning, I felt hurt, discouraged and hopeless. I could have waved the white flag of surrender, but something in me just couldn't let me. I had to keep going, to fight on and give it my best.

The point is this, which is what I told the lady, starting a business and building it into a great venture is not like making popcorn. It is not instant coffee. Starting any business needs a plan, persistence, intuition and what many call good luck while I call it God's leading.

Kenya's Bright Future

All the major indicators point to a bright future for Kenya. The nation is politically stable, the middle class is expanding, more and more Kenyans are getting educated at higher levels and the standard of living is rising. In spite of the many socio-political and economic problems we still face, it is clear that an environment now exists in Kenya and across Africa where those who are serious about business can thrive. The question is no longer whether big business can survive in Kenya, but how many young Kenyans will have the courage to start and nurture a business venture to success. The matter is no longer whether Mama Mboga-size businesses should be started, but how many are started to keep each of us busy at something productive.

It is because of my journey to the top in Kenya that I have a firm belief in the opportunities Africa has to offer her young people today. Don't wait for your uncle or aunt to get you a job or put you into an apprentice school, find a place where you can sit to think, to think about a credible business idea, then get out there and get started. If you fail, don't let that failure define your future. Dust up and learn from it, but keep going. That is the way to success!

In this book, I want to discuss with you the key elements you must consider in starting, running and expanding a business. You will interact with ideas on handling the social media for business, the power of teamwork, the place of vision, the structure of a company, marketing, innovation, time management and many other critical nuggets. By the time you are done reading this book there should no longer be a lingering question about your preparedness to start and run a business; the question should be when and where you launch the business—in Nairobi or in the counties?

The best place to begin this great discussion, therefore, is vision; because your vision will determine the overall direction and scope of your business. So what is vision and why should we care about it?

Questions

The questions hereunder are designed to review the key discussion points in this chapter. For deeper insights on this topic, readers are encouraged to study the matter broadly.

1. Define business.
2. On what basis does Kenya feature as a growing stable environment for business?
3. Who is Mama Mboga?

2 Vision

Vision is one of the most powerful words in business and perhaps in life as well. Many times I am tempted to think that the reason some people succeed in business while others fail is vision. Successful people have the ability to see clearly where they want to be five, ten or even twenty years from now. They are gifted with the ability to foresee the future and to make events today act in a choreographed fashion to drive toward achieving the goals that shape their vision.

Defining Vision

It is helpful that we define vision from the onset so that we know what we are working with. In business, vision is the ultimate dream. It is the place you, as the founder or manager of a business, wants it to be in a specified period of time and ultimately want to be when the goals you set out to achieve are finally curved like a rainbow in the deep horizon. If your ultimate goal in starting a business is, for example, to create employment for all the youth in your village and you have set systems in place to drive toward that reality in ten years, you could say it is a worthy vision. You could then go around the village satisfied that the building blocks for transforming the village are in place and that the possibility of a great community, anchored in the rule of law and gainful employment, is within sight.

At Optiven Ltd, our vision is to create one of Africa's leading real estate firms and to make it so friendly that virtually every son or daughter of Africa would want to own a home because of working with us. This is why our vision is bold, daring and urgent. It reads as follows: To be pacesetters in real estate across Africa. As you can see, that is not something one can imagine without looking deep in time and being brave enough to say *I am equal to the task*. It is a vision that fires us up!

It is crucial to understand, of course, that vision is like a mirage, it guides you and even makes you walk faster down the road to achieving it, but you never quite get to the end of it. A great vision is one that endlessly does that—it keeps you focused on the horizon, but you never quite get there. Take the example of the Kenya Airways vision: To be a world-class airline. Do you think that is something achievable? It is something at which KQ has to work for as long as it remains in business. It will never be achieved, but the lofty goal of achieving it keeps the airline company competitive and in top shape.

So should one have a vision before starting a business or after starting one? I have thrown this question in the mix early enough because it is a fundamental one. I want to give an answer to this critical question based on my own experience. I recall a time I was a marketing student at the University of Nairobi. I was already drawn to the business world and used a Yashika camera my brother bought me to take pictures of fellow students on campus and make a little money.

I was born into a poor home and was driven by the modest goal of building my mother a good house. The one in which she lived, after Dad was murdered, was leaning, dilapidated and could collapse under the weight of rains or strong winds from the Aberdares. Because of that goal, I used my Yashika to make money and paid for my upkeep in college, all along keeping my eye on the ball: to one day build mother a decent house. That goal formed and remained part of my vision to mold that village into a welcoming, conducive environment someday. It is the reason we have since registered Optiven Foundation to take poor children to school.

Power of a Vision

As you may have already sensed, vision is a powerful word that should evoke a sense of urgency, commitment and perseverance. It should make you feel captured by a force beyond your control, yet leave you sane enough to soberly plan and implement steps that when taken lead toward realization of key pillars of the vision. In life, it is the organizing principle that drives your life in the direction of giving you peace because you are fulfilling what you feel destiny placed you in the world to live for. When vision guides a life, inner peace follows!

To understand the role of vision and how powerful it is, there are key facts to consider:

a. **Who you are**. I have met men and women who wait till they turn fifty or sixty to begin a journey toward understanding themselves. In the United States, the term folks like that use is *to find myself*. That is just too late. To claim the ability to birth a vision and one day realize it, you must know who you are by understanding your temperament, intellect, abilities, endurance and other core character traits. Once you have that understanding, you may mold your abilities and gifts to fit in with your drive to live a vision.

Unleash Your Full Potential

b. **Credibility of your vision**. Credibility is a word that carries the same meaning as realistic or sensible. Does it sound sensible that Mama Mboga would go from selling vegetables to being a multimillionaire sports franchise owner in five years? Or does it sound credible that you should plan your purchase of land worth billions of shillings based on money you will make from winning a lottery? Vision is vision only when it is realistic and workable on the basis of resources one is capable of marshalling to realize it.

c. **Impact of vision**. The most critical test of any vision is the impact it has not only on the visionary, but on those the vision affects. If Bill Gates' and Steve Jobs' vision was to improve mankind's standard of living by creating computer software that packed unimaginable amounts of information into a tiny chip, the two gentlemen came a long way—perhaps beyond their wildest dreams. Any vision that falls short of having a positive impact on its originator and on the people it is meant to uplift their lives cannot be said to be a worthy one—and may in the end actually prove harmful and not a vision at all.

Is it possible, based on the foregoing discussion, for a business without a vision to survive and thrive? In rare cases yes, but a majority of businesses started without a vision or a plan will never get past a couple of months of existence. It is, therefore, necessary to spell out the vision so that stakeholders and workers—and all those tasked to implement it—may understand their roles.

Vision Statement

Coming up with a vision statement may sound like such a complicated thing to do, but what it means is that a vision, once formulated in someone's mind, should be written down in a coherent format so that whoever wishes to interrogate its elements or is tasked to implement them can refer to its core provisions as needed. From the Internet, let us look at two examples of vision statements, one from a trendy salon, the other from an online retailer.

> Our salon will change the way you think about a haircut. Full service comfort, friendly staff, a relaxing atmosphere, and the best prices in town give you an experience that will leave you glowing both inside and out.

It is clear from this vision statement what type of business is behind it. It is also a good, clear list of goals, without being too specific. It paints an overall picture of a pleasant, successful business that the company hopes to become, and since the vision statement isn't just a vision of your future, it is also a vision you are presenting to your customers about who you are; it is important that it does just that.

This next one is from a retail chain:

> We intend to provide our customers with the best online shopping experience from beginning to end, with a smart, searchable website, easy-to-follow instructions, clear and secure payment methods, and fast, quality delivery.

From this statement example, you can clearly tell that this company is an online retailer. You can also tell they have put thought into the statement by making a list of goals. They don't simply say that they want to be "the best" online shopping site, they give a list of ways in which they intend to do that. This is a quality vision statement because it outlines the specific future they intend to create for themselves, but it doesn't give specific steps on how they will do it (better saved for a mission statement).

To contextualize vision, it helps to consider the vision statement of one of Kenya's most successful companies. Equity Bank, under the visionary stewardship of one of Africa's greatest innovators, James Mwangi, has set the bar high and has been greatly rewarded by appreciative customers for its partnership with Kenyans and people across Africa. This is in keeping with its vision: To be the champion of the socio-economic prosperity of the people of Africa. Equity Bank makes it clear it will do whatever it takes to uplift lives in Africa. The element of fighting is enshrined in that vision, because indeed that is what it may take to uplift the lives of Africa's poor.

Another leading player in Kenya is Bidco. The company is run by my mentor, Vimal Shah. I admire the audacity of Bidco's vision statement.

Bidco will be the 1st African born, Africa-based transnational,
enjoying the loyalty of the Consumer Community.
Our products will touch common people, in a special way, on a daily
basis.
Profits will be ours and shall benefit all those who come in contact
with us.
We will be an African organization,
the world will benchmark with "The Bidco Way."
Our oils will lubricate our future growth.

That vision statement says everything one needs to know about Bidco's desire to play a positive role in Kenya, in Africa and around the world. That last line, that our oils will lubricate our future growth, plays into our definition of vision to the hilt. It points to the fact that the future will unfold guided by a great vision that will make Bidco competitive, and even the leader, but will remain something in the horizon—a great dream to pursue; a tantalizing aspiration!

When you enter most offices, you will see the vision displayed at a visible, central place. By that vision, you should be able to tell what the mission, core values and culture of the organization are—if they adhere to the vision. The vision dictates the manner in which all elements of an organization's running are harmonized to live its spirit. Indeed, when you look just beneath the surface of the vision statement, you should also be able to see in your mind's eye the mission statement.

Mission Statement

A mission statement is a statement that spells out who an organization is and how it intends to go about achieving its goals. It lays out, in broad generalities, the major steps an organization will take in an effort to reach its objectives and live its vision. Once again, let us take two examples of mission statements from the Internet of companies we know well.

> Our vision is to be earth's most customer centric company; to build a place where people can come

to find and discover anything they might want to buy online—from Amazon

To be customer centric and build a place where people can come to find and discover anything they might want to buy online is Amazon's goal. They will go about doing this by being and building. Being and building are general terms for a long list of actions Amazon will have to undertake to meet these goals.

The next mission statement is Apple's.

Apple designs Macs, the best personal computers in the world, along with OS X, iLife, iWork and professional software. Apple leads the digital music revolution with its iPods and iTunes online store. Apple has reinvented the mobile phone with its revolutionary iPhone and App Store, and is defining the future of mobile media and computing devices with iPad—from Apple.

The key words here are: designs, leads, reinvented and defining. These words paint in broad brushes a set of actions that Apple has to breakdown into activities that once done lead to the achievement of set goals. But once again, those set goals can only be achieved when a company adheres to core values that emerge and remain in harmony with the vision and mission.

Core Values

A company's core values are the guiding principles that its daily operations must abide by. Whereas many companies may display them as part of the mission statement, the best way to know and feel a company's core values is to experience the treatment you get when you visit. Where core values are displayed, what a client or customer expects is to be treated within the bounds of the values espoused and expressed by the company as its own and by which its officials and workers live.

The core values most companies espouse include:

- Dependable
- Reliable
- Loyal
- Committed
- Open-minded
- Consistent
- Honest
- Efficient
- Innovative
- Creative
- Motivated
- Positive
- Optimistic
- Inspiring
- Passionate
- Respectful
- Nurturing

As you have seen, core values are supposed to guide the behavior and actions in a company. They need to establish an atmosphere of predictability, harmony and the assurance of efficiency in production and quality in customer-relations. Any company that does not live by its declared core values is one nobody should expect any other element of management to be going right in because departure from core values is symptomatic of deeper malaise in the organization.

The question you may ask, having defined business as any venture started for the purpose of making money, is: does Mama Mboga or the matatu tout have core values? The answer is yes. The reason you will go to a certain Mama Mboga in your neighborhood and not others is because you have interacted with her and like her core values of respect, fairness and openness. You will also realize that there is a certain matatu that plies your route, which you like taking more than others. Again, it is because you like the core values of its touts and the discipline of the driver on the road.

It is important to realize that the core values you bring to the company will be a reflection of your personal values. If respect is your personal value, you will make it a core company value as well. It is, therefore, a great idea to reflect on your personal values and ensure they are in harmony with what society views as the ideal. Any company that internalizes and lives its core values eventually builds a solid culture.

Culture

Culture is the set way operations and the atmosphere in a company is expected to behave. Culture closely ties in with vision, mission and core values because it is a child of the union of the three. When a culture emerges that is strong and positive, a company grows faster and relates well with its environment, but when a negative culture is what emerges, there is no limit to the problems the company may face. Of course emergence of a negative culture should serve as a warning of departure from the vision and mission of the company.

Buying into the Vision

We close this discussion with this element because it is the hard part. As many company heads have discovered, it is easier to formulate a vision than to implement it. This is because implementation takes buying into the vision and mission of the company, which many workers never feel motivated to do—perhaps because they fail to see how the profits the company makes trickle down in a meaningful way to them.

A number of factors need to be considered in helping employees buy into the vision of an organization.

a. **Motivation**. This is the act of an employee feeling happy and fired up to carry out his or her duties to advance the vision and mission of the company—without coercion. An employee that is motivated will buy into the vision of a company because he or she sees the value of the company for self and for the community.

b. **Integrity**. Any company that hires workers who lack integrity is on its way to swimming in deep, troubled waters. When potential staff come to be interviewed for an advertised position in a firm, it is crucial to evaluate them on matters of integrity and pick only the man or woman who passes the integrity test. This is because when such a person says they will advance the vision and mission of the company, they mean just that. Their honesty is not in question.

c. **The bigger picture**. Employees will only buy into a vision they see as beneficial to them and to the community. To them, the bigger picture is what the presence of the company in the neighborhood means for the children, the youth and the elderly. If the net impact is positive, motivation becomes greater, but if the company exists solely to enrich a few, the sense of slaves toiling in a plantation sets in and vision suffers.

d. **Enthusiasm**. This is, perhaps, the most critical of all the factors to weigh in buying into a vision. Any great manager will want to ensure that his or her employees are not only motivated, but are truly enthusiastic about achieving the strategic goals of the company. Such enthusiasm is the product of: competitive remuneration, job security, a sense of being valued and wanted, and realization of the company's impact in the community where it is located.

As you may have already realized, we are keeping it practical. We have discussed the power of vision in a manner that anyone wishing to start a business can relate to. The ideas we have highlighted like spelling out a vision, spelling out a mission statement, having core values and developing a company culture are all crucial in living a vision. Now that we have established what vision is, in the next chapter we turn our attention to starting a business. What does it take to start one and how do you sustain the business venture?

Questions

The questions hereunder are designed to review the key discussion points in this chapter. For deeper insights on this topic, readers are encouraged to study the matter broadly.

4. Define vision.
5. What does it mean to buy into a vision?
6. Discuss:

    a. Mission statement.
    b. Company culture.
    c. Core values.

References

Website: www.bidco.co.ke

http://examples.yourdictionary.com/examples-of-core-values.html

https://www.facebook.com/Amazon/info

https://www.facebook.com/DeaShoppe/info

www.newvisionsinhair.com/#!untitled/

whatis.techtarget.com

3 Starting a Business

In my many travels in Kenya, across the region and all over the world, the one recurring question at forums has been: How does one start a business? What does it take to get it going and what does it take to sustain it? These are the key questions we want to grapple with in this chapter. As we already noted, anybody can start a business and even grow it into a major force for good, but should everybody start one? Should one be started merely for the sake of feeding a family or paying children's fees? The answers to these questions will surprise you and get you thinking about business in a manner you never have before.

If you talk to many business leaders today, there is every likelihood they will tell you that to start a business you need to begin by generating ideas. I won't quarrel with that approach, but I have found out, in my years as an entrepreneur, that the place to begin is having a passion for the line of business you want to get into. It follows, therefore, that we need to define passion and examine the role it plays in starting and sustaining a business. We must also discuss how to identify passion from a wish.

Defining Passion

If you were to wake me up in the middle of the night and asked what passion is, I would give you a straight, but irrelevant answer about passion being the sister of love. But if you asked me what it has to do with starting a business, I would have to ask you to meet me later in the day, preferably in my office, to talk seriously about the matter. I say so because in the realm of business, passion is everything. It is what keeps you going when the tide is high and the winds are blowing and your mind tells you to throw in the towel, but your heart tells you to give it just one more shot. That is passion.

Most dictionaries I have consulted relate passion to deep love or powerful sexual attraction—and they are right. I'm glad they bring up the matter of such intense love because that is the kind of love one needs to have before starting a business. This is important because business comes with enormous challenges and many times the temptation to give up stares one in the face, but if a business is anchored in deep love, a strong foundation of passion, the storms are easier to endure and manage.

It is, therefore, necessary to get *only* into the kind of business that you have very strong feelings for and may even be willing to die for. That kind of business is only possible because it harmonizes with your values, your mission in life and your desire to leave this world a much better place than you found it. It is driven by your gratitude to society for shaping you into what you are today and recognition that you are obligated to give back to society. Of course, nobody will come along and tell you that you are obligated to give back; you will feel it in your heart and the moment you start giving back, the sense will settle in that you have achieved passion in your business and are on a path to success.

It is this giving back which prompted us to start the Optiven Foundation, which has done a lot to make the world a better place to live. We operate on the premise that community work is part of our calling and we must have our eyes on the people. We have done water projects, educated the poor, supported orphans and undertaken other projects aimed at alleviating pain. The Foundation's goals and activities can be tracked on the website: www.optivenfoundation.org.

But, of course, the question many ask is how to tell what passion one has and how to align it with a business idea. For you to get a sense of how serious this is, we have to look at God's plan for each of us.

Identifying our Passions

In the biblical book of Ephesians 4:11-15, the Apostle Paul talks about the fact that the Lord Himself gave us key talents to use in this world for His glory. This is the same line of thought Pastor Rick Warren of Saddleback Church advances in his bestselling book *The Purpose Driven Life*. The Lord has given core gifts that He wants us to use and those core gifts or talents are what we must build our passions around. I feel it will serve us well to read those verses:

11And He gave some *as* apostles, and some *as* prophets, and some *as* evangelists, and some *as* pastors and teachers, **12**for the equipping of the saints for the work of service, to the building up of the body of Christ; **13**until we all attain to the unity of the faith, and of the knowledge of the Son of God, to a mature man, to the measure of the stature which belongs to the fullness of Christ. **14**As a result, we are no longer to be children, tossed here and there by waves and carried about by every wind of doctrine, by the trickery of men, by

Unleash Your Full Potential

craftiness in deceitful scheming; **15**but speaking the truth in love, we are to grow up in all *aspects* into Him who is the head, *even* Christ, **16**from whom the whole body, being fitted and held together by what every joint supplies, according to the proper working of each individual part, causes the growth of the body for the building up of itself in love.

Back when the Apostle Paul wrote those inspiring words to the Christians in Ephesus, the professional passions available for choice were limited indeed. If he were to write to the Christians in Nairobi or Kampala or Abuja or even Johannesburg, he would add to that list of God's gifting talents like:

a. **Healing**, where he would be talking about our medical doctors and nurses. Such folks have been given the ability to study medicine and play that great role Christ played when He was here: restoring wholesomeness (good health) in man. If this is your passion, wouldn't starting a business in healing be your calling?

b. **Teaching**, where he would be referring to our professors and lecturers and teachers. The Lord gave such folks the ability to hold the attention of others as they impart knowledge. Shouldn't such people start businesses in knowledge imparting ventures like nursery schools, primary schools and secondary schools? Even universities?

c. **Leadership**, where he would be meaning the gift of leading a people. The Lord has called certain folks to create peace and harmony around the world by leading others. Such people should start businesses geared toward enhancing peace in communities around the world.

These are but a few examples of how to match talents with a business passion. Of course there are those whose passion is to be pilots, fishermen, soldiers and even lawyers. The point is—all these talents and abilities are given so we can glorify God. If we, indeed, can see business as a tool put in our hands by the Creator for His glory, I have no doubt many of us will handle our business ventures in much the same way a pastor handles a church—as a mission entity. We will minister to the weak through the money we make; we will pay tithes on our earnings and expand the Kingdom of God through the profits our businesses generate.

—

I have observed, and maybe you have too, that as a child grows up, there are certain inclinations that make themselves revealed in the manner he or she does things. There will be children who even express those inclinations in the words: when I grow up I want to be_____. Have you heard them? What the child is expressing is the early signs of a passion. The child is telling the world what he or she already sees as the reason the Creator placed her in the world at this time and in this place. These are truly revolutionary thoughts. They cement our role in business as mere custodians of God's gifts, a fact that should keep us humble, focused and driven.

After one has established what his or her passion is, the next logical step is to select at least three best areas to start a business in.

Selecting Areas of Business

In recent days I've heard loud complaints about lack of great opportunities in Africa for the youth to exploit. Those complaints are due to the fact that the youth in America, Europe, Japan and other industrialized nations have greater, better opportunities to exploit. I agree that indeed that is the case, but what I disagree with is the notion that we should be crippled by lack of as many opportunities as our brothers elsewhere have. This continent has vast resources and opportunities for each one of us to interact with if we chose to. So what criteria should one use in selecting areas of business?

a. **Passion**. We have already discussed passion as the leading factor in starting and sustaining a business. If you don't have passion for what you are about to engage in, don't start!

b. **Inclination**. The reason this is key is because it is natural. Inclinations are never forced, they just happen. When you see a child carry a Bible and play a preacher all the time, you will know that the child is inclined in that direction and, if encouraged, will become a preacher. In like manner, if you see a child act militant and play a soldier, that may be his or her inclination unless dissuaded by an unimpressed father or mother.

c. **Subject choices**. This is an excellent indicator of what one desires to be and the good thing is, it always follows passion and inclination pretty closely. No student will have a passion for being a doctor yet end up studying geography; that just wouldn't make any sense.

d. **Mentorship**. The adult who chooses to mentor a youth will have seen a certain set of qualities that incline the youth to go in a given direction. A mentor would, therefore, do what it takes to help the youth be a doctor, teacher, nurse, lawyer or whatever he or she has judged to be the youth's talents.

Of course there are other indicators, but these are key and should be paid close attention to. Those who will succeed in business will be those who have paid attention to their talents, inclinations and the voice of their mentor. The greatest disservice we do ourselves is to start a business solely for the sake of making money and not for touching people's lives. We must come to the point where we see business as a ministry and handle it as such for it to grow and be a blessing.

—

Which brings me to this point. How does one zero in on just three ideas for business and eventually settle on one? This is a critical question because it is recognition of the fact that one is getting much closer to starting a business. If you have aligned your business thoughts with your passion, you should be getting pretty excited at this point because it begins to feel like a dream coming true. The days of wondering are over and you are about to make the first important decision of business: which business suits me? This can only be done if you have a formula to work with. That formula is nothing other than common sense. Let me explain by the use of a diagram. I call it the passion diagram.

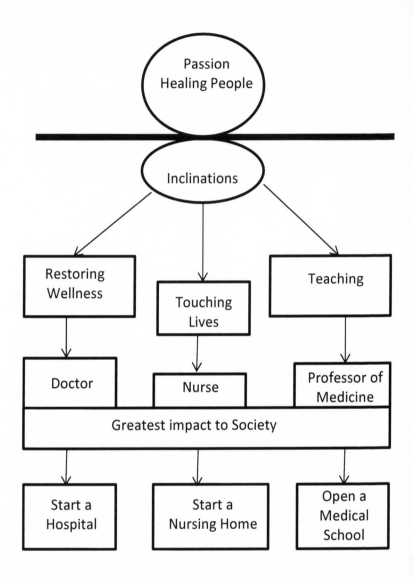

Figure 1.1 The Passion Diagram

This diagram illustrates the steps one needs to take in identifying that one business idea. It is a formula I would

Unleash Your Full Potential

love to see adopted by everyone interested in starting a business because it sieves the chaff and drops on your lap only that idea you have spent years searching for in your mind. It is like a magnifying glass that zeroes in on scattered thoughts in your mind and pulls out just one to magnify. Once your choice is wisely made, it is time to start generating ideas.

Idea Generation

In a later chapter, we will discuss innovation as a major player in business. I bring it up here because one might be tempted to confuse it with idea generation at this point. The difference between the two is that idea generation, at the point of starting a business, is meant to answer start-up questions, while innovation is for businesses that have already been in existence and are made more productive through injection of new ideas.

As you sit down to generate ideas, there are key areas you must look at because they are central to how quick and well your business takes off. I want us to discuss these areas one by one.

a. **Funding**. For many of us, this is where we hit a snag because we fear that nobody will advance us the capital to start a business. This fear is not unfounded. You have to be realistic and consider that banks and other lending institutions make their money only when loans are repaid and that can only happen when money is lent to someone who would use it to make more money. This being the case, alternative sources of funding must be sought. Don't let funding be a reason for you to stop dreaming about your business. Where there is a will, there is a way!

b. **Location**. If a business is to ever do well, it will have to be located at a suitable place. I started my business in an aging building somewhere in a scary part of Nairobi. I later realized that for people to take us seriously as a real estate firm, we had to move offices to Nairobi's CBD and rent better offices. We went from paying 8,000.00 shillings in rent to 500,000.00. This bold move paid off and now we are on top of our game. The point is—location is a critical factor. Make sure it is suitable for the nature of business you want to start, though. Don't think of starting a garage or a *nyoyo* and *uji* restaurant along Moi Avenue.

c. **Marketing**. This is one of the areas many folks fall flat. They assume that once a business is started customers will just come without marketing a product. The truth is—marketing is a core pillar in business and must be factored in as you think about starting one. When you market, a product moves; when you don't, a product does not move. There is no magic to it.

d. **Public relations**. This is the element I always refer to as the *forgotten key*. In most Management books, you will encounter a phenomenon called environment. Any business under the sun operates in a certain environment, which consists of an internal and external one. For your business to run well, a conducive atmosphere must be fostered and this is where public relations comes in. Don't ever let your business degenerate into an entity with a sour public image by ignoring the centrality of public relations in it.

e. **Giving back to community**. It is my experience that giving back to the community is a great tool in creating communal goodwill (public relations). The government has encouraged and legislated corporate responsibility as a requirement for firms in Kenya; which is the same thing as giving back to the community, but you will notice, if you care to look, that most corporations barely give anything commensurate to the profits they rake in; they give back peanuts. Let me whisper a secret: to whom much is given, much is expected.

f. **People or staff as a resource**. This is a key factor in business, but again it is one that most people overlook. As one starts a business, it helps to be aware of the nature of staff expected for success to be realized in the business. The idea is to match the right people with assignments they can handle with passion and ease.

Think Big, Start Small, Start Now

We are keeping it practical. At this stage you have thought things through and even rounded up a decent amount of money to start your business. There are thought-leaders who will tell you to come in roaring like a lion, but I would much rather that you come in meekly like a lamb. Starting small doesn't mean you don't know what you are doing, it means you are being cautious and feeling your way through the complex web of business. By starting small, you will:

- Control and have a better sense of cash flow,
- Adapt better to the environment by controlling the image you foster, and
- Have the joy of experiencing and knowing what growth is. If you start big, you may deny yourself that experience and expose yourself instead to negative growth—which could be discouraging.

The reason you have to start now is because it does not pay to procrastinate. Indeed, procrastination is a danger in business because while you wait, someone else with your line of thinking will implement the idea and deny you ownership of it. So once it is all systems go, pray about your ideas, gather the courage and start the business. The best time to get started is now!

As you get started, though, always think of the bigger picture. Set targets for yourself that you wish to meet. If you are an estate Mama Mboga, dream of becoming the leading supplier of that *mboga* to hotels in Nairobi. If you are vendor in Kampala or Maputo, set your mind on owning a supermarket in the city five or ten years from now. If you think big and keep a positive attitude about life, you will achieve your dreams in ways that will surprise even you. The idea is to remain focused.

—

When I was a poor student in Laburra, in Nyeri County, Kenya, my dream was to become a priest one day. As I grew up, however, and my eyes opened to the biting poverty and lack of opportunities in my village, I set my goals higher. I wanted to build my mom a better house and educate children who could not afford fees. It was at that time that I started to think big and organized my life to achieve my big dreams. In school I studied hard; at home I worked diligently; at church I played my role with dedication as an altar boy.

Later, when I came to Nairobi, I dreamt even bigger things. The possibilities seemed endless and I was eager to grab them, to take them and run with them. That was how I came to start a string of failed businesses before I finally got into real estate, where my company, Optiven Ltd, has been recognized as a leader in real estate. But we cannot sit on our laurels and say we have arrived; not at all, the dream is even bigger because we have now set our vision on becoming Africa's leading real estate organization. We are already exploring possibilities in Uganda, Tanzania and further afield in Rwanda and Burundi. With the opening up of the sizable East African Community to more nations, the market has expanded and possibilities are now endless. The time to think big in business is now; start small but rise to glory!

Questions

The questions hereunder are designed to review the key discussion points in this chapter. For deeper insights on this topic, readers are encouraged to study the matter broadly.

1. Define passion.
2. What is the meaning of idea generation?
3. Discuss key elements of the passion diagram.

References

Warren, R. (2008). *The Purpose Driven Life.* Zondervan.

Website: www.learnersdictionary.com/definition/passion

www.optivenfoundation.org

4 Marketing

Many people who are not well prepared discover, as I did, that once a business is started, marketing is the next big thing. I recall my days at the University of Nairobi, where my business revolved around taking images of fellow students with my Yashika camera. The name of the business was Wamu Holdings, under which I ran Capturing the Moment. It did not take me long, after starting it, to realize that as many people on campus as possible needed to know about my camera and its amazing abilities. Those were the days when taking a nice picture at Uhuru Park or at the KICC or any known part of Nairobi earned you fame when the picture was shown to folks back in the village.

My immediate concern, therefore, was how to market my small business. In this chapter, I want to share down-to-earth, practical ideas about marketing; but I will also share other ideas larger companies use because you will one day want to know them after your young company has expanded and finally plays in the big league. The progression of size goes something like this:

a. **Mama Mboga**. This is a very basic level at which marketing is essential, but can be accomplished with minimum or no money at all.

b. **Small and Medium-sized Enterprises (SMEs)**. Like Optiven Ltd, this is a sizable, significant operation that needs serious marketing and must engage a budget for this purpose that is equal to the task of marketing its products well.

c. **National organization**. Like Kenya National Oil Corporation or Kenya Cooperative Creameries, this is a national business that can only reach target customers by marketing on national media. This involves a huge budget because reaching the four corners of a nation is not a small matter.

d. **Multinational organization**. A good example of a Kenyan business that has gone multinational is Nakumatt, which operates vibrant stores in Kenya, Uganda, Tanzania, Rwanda and is set to open stores in other nations in the region. When a business gets this large, marketing is high stakes and involves a lot of money. The personnel brought in to handle marketing must be men and women of great knowledge in this area.

e. **Global conglomerate**. These are the Hewlett-Packards of this world; the broadcasting brands like CNN and even global churches like the Catholic Church. This is a dizzying level at which marketing is no longer just about products, but involves a certain level of diplomacy—and may indeed take the chairman of the conglomerate along with the marketing head. If, for example, CNN wished to get into China in the eighties, it would have had to take Ted Turner himself to sit with the leadership of that nation.

The discussion we have had above is critical to the under-standing of marketing. It sets the stage for us to have a realistic picture as a business takes off. Because of the graduated levels we have listed, it is only fair that we look at marketing ideas that suit the smaller businesses before we get into the more complex operations.

Marketing with Zero Capital

In the many seminars and workshops I've moderated, people drop jaws in disbelief when I say marketing can be achieved with zero capital. Of course they do because I always wait to tell them what level of business I have in mind. It would be too costly for Mama Mboga or even small shops to engage capital in marketing. These are the businesses that need to make great use of the zero capital approach to marketing. Let us consider them:

Word of Mouth

This is one of the most effective tools in marketing for a small operation like a shop or Mama Mboga. A savvy business person will know how to send word in the street and throughout the estate about the quality, speed of service and affordability of products. As this is done, it helps to be well groomed and cheerful. Customers don't like to go to a person with a long face especially after they have had a long day at work or in the field.

Be aware, as a trader in an estate or street, that most of the folks who buy from you will be house-helps. Those folks are some of the most powerful word-of-mouth agents you'll ever meet anywhere. A friend of mine calls them estate journalists because when they congregate, they gossip and discuss everything going on in each home in the estate. They also know who the good Mama Mboga is, the best hair stylist is, the kind doctor is and even who the most loving pastor is. Make the house help your ally in putting out a positive word about your business for you.

Keep in mind too that your ultimate goal in the business is to grow it; and so as you project that positive image, let your customers know that growth is on your mind. Whisper your plans to them and let them feel part of the great successes you will achieve with their help.

Business Cards

Business cards are an essential tool in marketing. In today's world, a serious business person will want to have his or her card wherever he or she is to tell about the nature and location of the business. Your very first indication of lack of seriousness is lack of that card. If you came to me and told me you sell cars or own a shop at the corner in my estate, I would want a card to act as the initial verifier of your claims. Should there be none, chances are I will not even bother to follow up and you will have lost me just like that.

A well-presented business card should contain the following basic information:

a. **Name of business**. This is the *actual* name your business goes by and by which it exists in the government's registry of businesses in the nation. If, by any chance, your customers have given the business another "great" name as a matter of endearment, you can slide that name on the card in brackets—next to the actual name.

b. **Your name and title**. Let your customers know your actual name and title in the business. If you are the owner say so. And again, if a name of endearment has been added to you by appreciative customers, you may bracket it on the side of your real name.

c. **Address and phone number**. This is important because it tells your customers, and all those who might be interested in your products, where to find you. In case they fail to locate you, having a phone number on the card will help because they will call and ask where to find you.

d. **Product list, website, email address, Twitter handle**. A product list is a customer's first glance at what you offer. It should be quick, brief and to the point. If they wish to find out details, the website will provide that. It also helps to have your email address and Twitter handle on the card so that folks who prefer to communicate in either of those platforms are not disadvantaged.

There are people out there who generate colorful and childish cards indeed; you will soon meet them. Your card should be simple, appropriate and welcoming, not a piece of embarrassing artwork that when you present to anyone, they would blush and never want to associate with you. Here is a sample of my card:

Figure 2.2 Card sample

Before I close this segment, there is a need to warn that certain businesses are so sensitive that giving an exact address may put you in danger. For example, a private eye or a crime buster or an investigative freelance reporter may not wish to be placed at a certain fixed

Unleash Your Full Potential

location for fear of being murdered or harmed by those whose crimes he or she is investigating. This is a matter each of us has to consider as we assess the nature and security of the business we are engaged in.

Referrals

Referrals are from people who know you well because you have interacted at a certain level. They may be people you go to church with, people your children go to school with their children, people you work with who know the nature of your business or customers who had a pleasant experience when you served them. When a person is referred to you, they will expect high quality service because they rely on the good word of the referee—a person they trust. Imagine what it says about the referee when you mishandle the person they sent to you; it is the equivalent of saying: *That guy who sent you to me was such a liar, I'm not that great!*

Treat each customer and any other person who walks through the door of your business with dignity. Offer a smile and be of assistance even when it seems like they are merely window-shopping. This may well be the reason American businesses coined the phrase *customer is always right*. If you don't treat a customer well and they happen to have been referred to you, not only won't they buy from or deal with you, but they will neither refer anyone else nor hesitate to discourage those who want to seek your services.

Social Media

This is a broad area that could form the basis for another book, but for the purposes of this discussion, we will highlight only the aspects that apply within the scope of this narrative. My favorite definition of social media is the one on *WhatIs.com*. Here it is:

> Social media is the collective of online communications channels dedicated to community-based input, interaction, content-sharing and collaboration. Websites and applications dedicated to forums, microblogging, social networking, social bookmarking, social curation, and wikis are among the different types of social media.

Among the most used social media platforms are:

- Facebook,
- Twitter,
- Instagram,
- LinkedIn, and to an extent
- Websites.

In recent days, I have seen no less a business magnate than Sir Richard Branson, the CEO of Virgin Atlantis, use Facebook to communicate. I have also noted that President Barack Obama and President Uhuru Kenyatta have vibrant Facebook accounts that update citizens. This is crucial because social media has emerged as, perhaps, the most popular way for humankind to pass time. Those who are keen on global trends are already aware that you meet parishioners, citizens and most customers on Facebook, on Twitter, on LinkedIn and the websites; folks hardly ever come to gatherings anymore.

There are no hard-and-fast rules to engage the social media in creative marketing, but certain common sense approaches are critical. We view these approaches in light of the fact that social media is more of a place for folks to hang out rather than be bombarded with adverts and facts about products. Being creative and innovative is, therefore, key to how people will react to invading their space and asking for a bit of their time.

Among the key elements you want to keep right are:

a. **Language**. Any social media platform is much like a bus, where all kinds of people will get in and say whatever they want to say. A business person, however, has no such luxury. The language of a business person must be polite, polished and engaging. The nature of social media is such that there are a number of competing attractions in messages, images and ideas that compete for attention; to hold the interest of potential clients, one's language has to be top-notch.

b. **Speed of response**. This is one of the areas people fail as businessmen or women. There are folks out there who wait a bit too long to answer the questions of clients either because they are *busy*, *away* or *engaged*. To a customer, such lateness in response is indicative of lack of seriousness and may be the reason a deal is not struck. Always be sure to engage your customers and potential clients quickly, efficiently and with as much of helpful information as they require.

c. **What to look at**. We already noted earlier that social media is like a bus. Not everyone in the bus is good for your business; in fact many folks there may be harmful to the business. Be careful how you pick the people you target as potential customers. Look carefully at their profile, the folks who are their friends, the nature of what they write and the kinds of interests they have. An assessment of these elements should provide a clear indication of the nature of person the potential target is.

d. **Lead generators of interest**. Lead generators refer to those images, words and one-liners that will pique the interest of a potential customer. As a business person, be sure to place on Facebook, your website and other forums images of your products, your catchy one-line phrases and words that are bound to make people stop and linger just long enough to get your message.

Electronic and Print Media Campaign

It has been the case in Kenya that whenever we talk about electronic and print media we mean radio and television. The nature of marketing that involves this kind of medium is serious in budget, purpose and is expected to draw in hefty profits. In the last couple of years, Kenya has liberalized her airwaves, a factor that has enabled television stations to go from the dominant Kenya Broadcasting Corporation of the one party era to more than five—and growing. The stations are:

- **Citizen TV**, which has the largest viewership and retains the ability to grow even more dominant. It is watched by millions of Kenyans because of its dynamism in programming, which enables it to reach all segments of the Kenyan society.

- **Nation TV**, which is just as innovative and rich in programming, but reaches a segment of Kenya that tends to be middleclass. The target audience for NTV adverts is, thus, the middle to upper class Kenyans.
- **Kenya Television Network (KTN)**, which is the third largest station in Kenya and cuts both ways in programing, reaching the lowly and the mighty in equal share.

There are other networks like GBS, Qtv, KISS, K-24 and a myriad of others on DStv. This class of stations is geared toward a narrower (niche) segment of viewer-ship. For example, KISS scratches the itch for popular culture, Qtv speaks to the needs of the younger demographic, while K-24 speaks to the interests of an urban youth. If one is to advertise in any of these networks, it has to be niche advertising, targeting only that particular demographic or interest group.

Radio, perhaps because it is easier to set up, has been even broader in its liberalization and now reaches Kenyans in greater numbers than ever before. There are vernacular stations all across the country and each one reaches a sizable population of Kenyans. The most influential ones, however, remain those that target

Kenya's largest ethnic groups like the Kikuyu, Luo, Luhya, Kalenjin, Kisii and Kamba.

For maximum impact, one needs to choose carefully the radio station to market in because it costs a lot of money to run even a thirty-second clip. The bottom line in these adverts is that they should generate buzz and lead to greater income generation.

Talk Big, Believe you are Big

This is a great place to end this chapter. My experience in Kenya is that nobody wants to associate with small things. Learn to project your business as aggressive and set to become the next Nakumatt or Equity. Make the people you interact with take you seriously. Had I not learnt this lesson early enough, I probably would not have propelled Optiven Ltd to such great heights.

As you engage in big talk, though, be sure to keep your word, to maintain your integrity and to remain credible. Don't make grandiose claims that when one weighs they find ridiculous. For example, it would be unwise for me to walk up to a group of young people and claim to be the President's physician. First of all, I'm not a doctor; and second, finding out who the President's doctor is wouldn't be such a difficult task. Lies and exaggerations are an unhealthy way of going about things because sooner or later they expose you to ridicule and loss of customers. Keep it straight—but talk big, big, big!

Questions

The questions hereunder are designed to review the key discussion points in this chapter. For deeper insights on this topic, readers are encouraged to study the matter broadly.

1. Define marketing.
2. What are the key ways an entrepreneur can market with zero capital?
3. Discuss the role of the social media in marketing.

References

Website: www.Georgewachiuri.com

www.WhatIs.com

5 Organizational Structure

Structure has emerged as one of the main aspects of business management in recent years. All over the world, business leaders have sought to have deeper understanding and complete control of the operational structure of the organizations they run. This is because such intimate understanding enables them to put in place commensurate levels of accountability and create manageable bureaucracy. Small and medium-sized enterprises will, of course, have leaner structures while global conglomerates like Hewlett-Packard will have fairly complex ones. Regardless of the size of a business, however, it is critical that for smooth operations to become integrated within the fabric of a firm's culture, an organogram be set in place that all employees of the company are exposed to and can understand.

Defining Organogram

I like the *Wikipedia* definition of organogram, which others call organigram, organization chart or org chart. It says that an organogram is a diagram showing graphically the relation of one official to another, or others, of a company. It is also used to show the relation of one department to another, or others, or of one function of an organization to another, or others. This chart is valuable in that it enables one to visualize a complete organization by means of the open picture it presents.

A company's organizational chart will typically illustrate relations between people within an organization. Such relations might include managers to sub-workers, directors to managing directors, chief executive officer to various departments and so forth. When an organization chart later grows too large it can be split into smaller charts for separate departments within the organization. The different types of organization charts include:

- Hierarchical,
- Matrix, and
- Flat (also known as Horizontal)

There is no accepted form for making organization charts other than putting the principal official, department or function first, or at the head of the sheet, and the others below, in the order of their rank. The titles of officials, and sometimes their names, are enclosed in boxes or circles. Lines are generally drawn from one box or circle to another to show the relation of one official or department to the others. In short, it is all about relations!

Scholars and thought-leaders in the field of management will probably have a more complex definition of the term, but for the purposes of this book, the *Wikipedia* definition will suffice. It spells out the major levels of a business hierarchy that need to be in an organogram. Before we discuss those levels and their roles, we need to look at a sample organogram, an illustrative one that will capture the administrative levels of a company.

OPTIVEN LTD ORGANOGRAM (Figure 2.3)

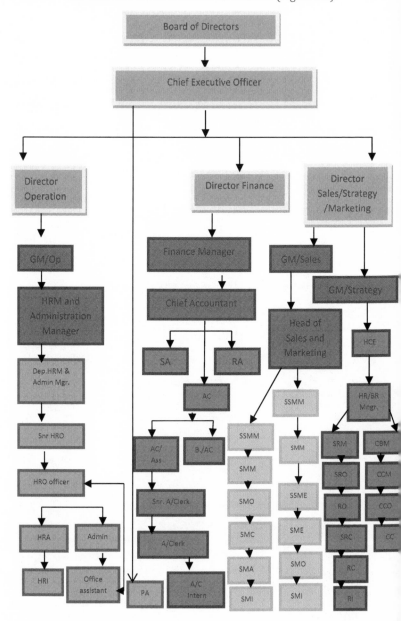

Manager

As you can see from the illustrative diagram above, the top level of any organization is occupied by the office that oversees all operations of the company. In most companies, the officer in this top office is called a Manager, but could be referred to in others as Executive Director, Chief Executive Officer and any other terms connoting authority.

A Manager and the deputies are expected by the Board of Directors of a company, if it is a large enough operation, to ensure that all systems of the company work in coordinated harmony to maximize output and ensure compliance with the company's strategic objectives, goals and vision. The expectation is that when all systems work for a common purpose, the company's profits will soar and relations with its environment will be harmonious.

In smaller units like a corner shop or the Mama Mboga type of operation, the Manager may also serve as the Treasurer, the Public Relations Officer and any other position his small business requires him or her to fill. When we started Optiven Ltd I occupied all these positions and I can't tell you enough how exhausting it was. This is the reason one needs to think carefully about starting a business, because without passion for it, when the times get incredibly tough, as they surely will, discouragement and fear will kill it.

Financial Controller

This is one of the most powerful positions in a company and should be handled by a professional with vision, strategy and innovativeness. This is the official expected to ensure that the financial books of a company are sound, that cash flow is handled with care and that all debts and debtors are factored into budgets and profits.

Executive Secretary

This is the company official expected to handle all matters of records. In most organizations this is the person tasked to handle matters of policy and must be well versed in matters of the nation's labor laws—and other regulatory statutes of a nation. In the event that a company is large enough to hire a lawyer, the lawyer and the Executive Secretary have to work in close consultation to keep the company on sound legal and ethical footing.

—

The other officials of a company are lower in ranking, but are no less important. Any company that will achieve its strategic objectives and move toward its vision is one that has created an internal environment that honors the place of each employee—from the janitor to the Chief Executive Officer. Though an organogram rates, in descending order, the place of each company employee, it is crucial for the top leadership to foster communal approach to problem-solving and make each employee feel wanted and appropriately valued.

Systems

In business, a system is a methodical procedure or routine used to deliver set goals. A system comprises of inputs and outputs that are measurable and all its parts influence other parts of it. In the event that any aspect of a system dysfunctions, the harmonious coexistence of parts in the entire system may be rendered broken and in need of repair for normalcy to resume.

The term homeostasis is used to refer to a state of affairs where balance and harmony are achieved despite changing circumstances in the environment. A company must work to create systems that purposefully galvanize for the sake of living the vision of the organization. When all systems work together, they produce a super system or culture, which is in turn responsible for creating the company's internal environment (a complex whole). That is the system.

—

At the back of your mind you are probably beginning to wonder where we dropped off Mama Mboga and the small shop owner. The complex structures and elements of business we are discussing now are our way of saying the small business we have been discussing since the beginning of this book has now grown and evolved into an organization with robust systems, a fully-developed organogram and a credible budget.

Optiven Ltd started small, just like others. As I said earlier, I recall the time I was the manager, accountant, sales person, messenger and played all other roles as needed. Five years down the line, an old friend, who had been following Optiven activities on the media, walked into our head office at Barclays Plaza, 14th floor, Loita Street, Nairobi, and asked what we had done to be so successful in such a short span of time.

His words were, "George, how did you make it to the top so fast? How did yours become Kenya's best overall company under the Mid-sized Companies Award 2014/15 and the best in Real Estate/Property and Construction 2014/2015?"

"Come with me, I want to show you something," I said.

As we walked along, he told me that he had read my bestselling book *Soaring Like An Eagle* and had been a follower on my Facebook (George Wachiuri). He had also become an ardent reader of the daily posts on my blog www.Georgewachiuri.com.

I took my friend to a water tap on the 14th floor. I turned on the faucet and water started running. I said, "How is it that this water has made it to the 14th floor?"

He looked at me in deep thought, then offered several suggestions: There must be a water tank on top. There must be a pump on the ground floor. There could be an internal tank. And on he went...

"No, no and no," I told him. "It's none of those!"

I finally gave him the answer. "The water flows well because of excellent plumbing work."

He shrugged. "And your point?"

"In business the CEO is a chief plumber who must trust in God, facilitate good systems, great policies, strategy, communication structure, work well with people, coach, train, hire right people, develop leaders around him or her, deliver on promises made, delegate responsibility, promote good culture, and ensure systems that support customers. When all these are in place, the process of growth is set on autopilot mode."

"Good plumbing?" he asked, weighing my words as if I had just become a maharishi. "That's what it takes?"

I said, "Good plumbing is the reason Optiven Ltd is on the right vision and will one day appear on the Forbes List of companies that have achieved transformation in people's lives, that is the best organization to work for, that is a company which makes the world a better place to live in, that is the most innovative, and that is a pot for idea generation."

"Amazing!"

"You are right," I said. "Optiven is moving firmly in the direction of leaving a positive mark in the world. The answer is GOOD PLUMBING!"

Policies

In a company, policies are a written set of principles and procedures formulated and adopted by the company to foster an environment that leads to realization of its strategic goals. In general, policies are adopted by the board of an organization while procedures are adopted by senior executive officers.

Because policies are the core framework upon which an organization's decisions are made, it is always critical for organizations to have a policy document that all can refer to. A well-developed policy is one that answers basic questions about its existence—it contains certain standard components that define it as thought-out; not just a set of procedures shoved down employees' throats for the sake of maximization of profits alone. Among the standard components are:

a. **A purpose statement**, outlining why the company is issuing the policy, and what its desired effect is, or what its outcome should be.

b. **An applicability and scope statement**. This is a statement that describes who the policy affects and which actions are impacted by the policy. The applicability and scope may expressly exclude certain people, certain firms, and certain actions from the policy requirements. Applicability and scope is used to focus the policy on the desired targets only, and avoid unintended consequences where possible.

c. **An effective date which indicates when the policy comes into force**. Retroactive policies are rare, but can be found.

d. **A responsibilities section,** indicating which party or parties and organizations are responsible for carrying out individual policy statements. Many policies may require the establishment of some ongoing function or action. For example, a purchasing policy might specify that a purchasing office be created to process purchase requests, and that this office be responsible for ongoing actions.

e. **Policy statements that indicate the specific regulations, requirements, or modifications to organizational behavior the policy is creating**. Policy statements are extremely diverse depending on the organization and intent, and may take almost any form.

There are certain policies that may go a step further and contain additional sections, including:

- Background, indicating any reasons, history, and intent that led to the creation of the policy, which may be listed as motivating factors. This information is often quite valuable when policies must be evaluated or used in ambiguous situations, just as the intent of a law can be useful to a court when deciding a case that involves that law.
- Definitions, providing very clear and unambiguous definitions for terms and concepts found in the policy document (*Wikipedia*).

To conclude this chapter, it is important to make it clear that there is no one formula for drawing up a structure of a company. The best way to go about formulating a structure is to harmonize the role of the company with the environment it finds itself in. In other words, if the company is a community hospital, its organizational structure should be reflective of the core roles it plays in the community. The strength and budget of each office should reflect those very roles.

After a company's structure is put in place, however, it is wise to deliberate on short and long-term strategies that would lead to achieving the vision. In the next chapter we want to discuss the role of strategic planning in achieving a company's strategic objectives and goals.

Questions

The questions hereunder are designed to review the key discussion points in this chapter. For deeper insights on this topic, readers are encouraged to study the matter broadly.

1. What is organogram?
2. Define the core roles of a company's top executives.
3. What is a budget?

References

Website: www.Georgewachiuri.com

en.wikipedia.org/wiki/Organizational chart

6 Strategic Planning

Strategic planning has emerged as perhaps the most important element of a company. Seeing how core a player it has become, it is surprising that in the past, it was not a factor in business and waited to emerge in the sixties, when certain private corporations took a second look at the military concept of strategy and adopted it as a helpful approach in planning. Since the 1960s, thus, strategic planning has been studied and fine-tuned by researchers to make it a central plank in management. Because of the weighty nature of this chapter, we will rely heavily on literature past and present.

Defining Strategic Planning

You have undoubtedly noted that we have left behind the basic approaches suitable to start-ups and are now playing in the realm of businesses that have taken off and are running with a sense of direction. Because of this new approach, strategic planning cannot be defined in a pedestrian manner at this stage. To be fair to the weight of its importance, we have to look at what key researchers in the emerging field have adopted as the most appropriate definition of the concept.

One of the leading voices in strategic planning in the recent past is a scholar B.J. Burnside (2002). After a thorough study of this concept, he came up with a definition that was widely accepted and prevailed for a long time. He said:

> Strategic planning is the process of determining the mission, objectives, strategies and policies that govern the acquisition and allocation of resources to achieve organizational goals or aims.

This definition, as is reflected in its inclusive nature, was a product of years of studying the concept. Scholars like Burnside wanted to conclusively understand the many dynamics involved in strategy and how they affected management. Earlier, in 1994, two other scholars had defined it as:

A means to an end, a method used to position an organization through prioritizing its use of resources according to identified goals in an effort to guide its direction and development over a period of time.

The two definitions, taken together, are what strategic planning is about. Here in Kenya, and all across Africa, the concept has finally caught on and many organizations have made it a requirement for management. Even the government, aware of the enormous role strategy plays in maximizing output, has adopted strategic planning and made it a requirement for contracting. All ministries and state corporations, as part of a contractual obligation with the government, must have a strategic plan that harmonizes with the economic blueprint adopted by the Kibaki government known as Vision 2030. Under this vision, Kenya is supposed to rise from a third world economy to an industrialized one.

Looking at the measurable gains Kenya has experienced in the economic sector since the inception of the Vision 2030 strategy, it is evident that strategic planning is key to growth. And it is not as complex an issue as certain professionals make it out to be; there are only three key parts to it, which are what Hopkins and Hopkins (1997) identified. These are:

- Formulation
- Implementation and
- Control

Formulation

This is the process of coming up with a coherent plan that takes into account the vision of the company. It is at this stage that a company's strategic objectives and goals are developed and harmonized with its vision. Scholars are agreed on the fact that formulation of strategy is normally the easy part because all it takes is for professionals to sit and think things through, giving dates and assigning roles to officials and employees of the company. In essence, it is coming up with a roadmap. In Kenya, as in most of Africa, organizations outsource the formulation of strategy to professionals in the field and even bring them in to train staffers on it once it is formulated. This is the reason you sometimes see employees of a company bused into Mombasa or some other town and kept for three to five days to be trained on the vision, strategic objectives and goals of the company. The expectation is that once trained, these employees should go back with renewed vigor to do the actual task of implementing the strategy.

Implementation

Implementation is the process of actualizing the plan. This is the doing part. At this stage, the party is over and work must be done for the vision to be realized. For this to happen, top management, all employees and all other stakeholders must buy into the vision and strategic objectives of the company and be enthusiastic about implementing them. What we have observed in Africa, though, has been lack of commitment on the part of top managers to take responsibility for implementation of the plans, especially in the public sector. Private firms, purely driven by profit considerations and market share, are a lot more attuned to implementation.

If you were to ask me what implementation therefore means in pedestrian terms, I would say it is following the strategy laid down by the trainers who walked you through the company's strategic plan. It is doing what your managers ask you to do, assuming they have perfectly understood the plan. Because that clear understanding and commitment lacks sometimes, certain challenges may result. As Fleming and other scholars (2005) have observed, and as magnified by Odundo (2012), those challenges include:

a. **A top-down and laissez faire management style**. This is what ails most corporations, most of which are in the public sector. In the private sector, managers are expected to be skilled and driven to achieve the vision and maximize output for the company. Any manager who fails to show results and adhere to a company's core vision is a candidate for removal.

b. **Unclear strategic intentions and sorely conflicting priorities**. Though this may be blamed in part on formulators of the strategy, the buck must stop with the management, those who failed to source for qualified professionals to formulate a strategy that would achieve the firm's vision.

c. **An ineffective senior management team**. Again this is an acuter problem in the public than in the private sector. Still, even in private companies there are managers who have no clue what they are doing and may have been brought in by relatives or friends. The problem of nepotism and tribalism is a key factor exacerbating this situation.

d. **Lack of rewards system**. Most businesses are afflicted in this respect because they have failed to put in place policies that guide rewarding good performance. What this says is that most firms in Kenya do not appreciate their workers. A work force that is not motivated will not deliver on your vision—what's in it for them?

The final aspect of strategic planning, and perhaps the most crucial, is control or measures. In the world of strategic planning, this is what certain scholars have referred to as strategic situational diagnosis. This is a big phrase that simply means assessing, from time to time, the implementation of a strategic plan. It presupposes that target dates and target goals were set in place when the plan was formulated. These targets are the ones that guide those tasked to assess how well or poorly a firm is implementing its strategy and is the basis upon which changes and adjustments may be made to focus the drive to vision achievement better.

Why Strategic Planning?

This is a question many organization heads have asked whenever they are faced with a need to lay strategy for the firms they lead. At Optiven Ltd, I recall the first time a professional strategist walked into my office and spent nearly an hour trying to sell me the idea of having a strategic plan for the company. I had not read as broadly as I have today and was too new to this level of business to see any meaningful link between strategy and performance. I did not know that Optiven had grown to a point where strategic planning was now a necessity.

Liou (2000) is probably the scholar who has listed the reasons for strategic planning better than any other. He says it is critical to impellent strategic plans to:

- **Think strategically**. It is important to wake up each day with a clear sense of purpose, guided by the vision of the company. Each day should serve as another push toward achieving an objective and bringing the company closer to its goals.

- **Clarify future direction**. It is amazing that firms in the past got away with the sin of having no strategic plans. I don't know how they made it— maybe they were not as complex and as far-flung in borders as today's multinationals and global conglomerates are. To have that credible sense of direction, an organization must have objectives, clear goals and a vision. That vision can only be realized when a defined strategy is in place and each company employee understands it.

- **Solve threatening organizational problems and improve performance**. This is only possible because when strategy acts as a roadmap, it is easy to tell when a wrong exit has been taken and the car is headed in the wrong direction.

- **Build teamwork and expertise**. Teamwork is only possible to build when employees understand what the vision is and what their core role in living it is. When employees don't know what they are required to do confusion sets in and frustration later harms performance. Strategy, as a roadmap, eliminates this problem.

Liou (2000) goes on to warn that a strategic plan should not be cast in stone, but should be treated as a flexible organism that guides toward a vision. What this means is that a great strategic plan should steer a company in the direction of dealing safely with rapidly-changing circumstances. It should not act as a doctrinal document whose fixed tenets cannot be altered under whatever circumstance; indeed that would give it away as a liability and not an asset to the organization.

Role of Environment

Many strategic planners never realized, until much later, the prominent role a company's environment played in performance. Today it is accepted by scholars across the board that a company has:

a. **An internal environment**, which develops and evolves into its culture. An internal environment consists of the documented and unspoken rules that guide the affairs of the company from within. A company's management has a free hand to make changes should that internal environment be in need of stabilization.

b. **An external environment**, which develops and evolves into the public image of the company in the community where it is located. In most cases, a firm's managers are limited in what they can do to alter that external environment, especially where it deals with matters implemented at a legislative level in Parliament.

Political Environment

It wouldn't be right to complete this segment on the environment without making tacit reference to politics. In Africa, as in much of the rest of the world, politics dictates the direction of policy and regulations that govern business. In Kenya, we have had our fair share of political upheavals that have affected the environment in which our companies do business. In the recent past, though, Kenya has stabilized and growth has been experienced in all sectors.

For us to continue on a path to stability, we have to insist on being governed democratically, with critical institutions like a free press, a vibrant Parliament and an independent Judiciary fostered. These are the main pillars of a stable nation, one where an environment for business is encouraged and people are not afraid to invest in.

SWOT Analysis

Ending such a spirited discussion on strategic planning without mentioning SWOT analysis wouldn't be a great idea. To understand the role of SWOT analysis in planning, consider that it is the way a company assesses its Strengths, Weaknesses, Opportunities and Threats. It is only after those SWOTs are assessed that a strategic plan can be formulated and later implemented. The reason I did not open this discussion with SWOT analysis is because I did not want our focus drawn away from the role of strategic planning in a company's performance.

As we discuss SWOT analysis, we should not lose sight of the fact that for a mature organization, SWOT analysis should always be conducted first, then a fitting strategy formulated to answer the assessment of the analysis. So, what is SWOT analysis?

Defining SWOT Analysis

In my research on this matter, I have consulted books and other forms of literature, but by far the best definition I have come across on this subject matter is right there in *Wikipedia*. A SWOT analysis or a SWOT matrix is a structured planning method used in the assessment of strengths, weaknesses, opportunities and all threats involved in a project or in a business venture. A SWOT analysis can be carried out for a product, place, industry or person. It involves specifying the objective of the business venture or project and identifying the internal and external factors that are favorable and unfavorable to achieve that objective. Some authors credit SWOT to Albert Humphrey, the man who led a convention at the Stanford Research Institute (now SRI International) in the 1960s and the 1970s using data from Fortune   500 companies. However,   Humphrey himself does not claim the creation of SWOT, and the origins remain obscure. The degree to which the internal environment of the firm matches with the external environment is expressed by the concept of strategic fit.

- **Strengths**: characteristics of the business or project that give it an advantage over others.
- **Weaknesses**: characteristics that place the business or project at a disadvantage relative to others.
- **Opportunities**: elements that the project could exploit to its advantage.
- **Threats**: elements in the environment that could cause trouble for the business or project.

That brief definition will suffice. Before we look at key aspects of this analysis, let us look at a simple example of a SWOT analysis. The diagram below, drawn from the internet, will serve that purpose.

Unleash Your Full Potential

Strengths	Weaknesses
• **Knowledge:** Our competitors are pushing boxes. But we know systems, networks, programming, and data management. • **Relationship selling:** We get to know our customers, one by one. • **History:** We've been in our town forever. We have the loyalty of customers and vendors.	• **Price and volume:** The major stores pushing boxes can afford to sell for less. • **Brand power:** We can't match the competitor's full-page advertising in the Sunday paper. We don't have the national brand name.
Opportunities	**Threats**
• **Training:** The major stores don't provide training, but as systems become more complex, training is in greater demand. • **Service:** As our target market needs more service, our competitors are less likely than ever to provide it.	• **The larger price-oriented store:** When they advertise low prices in the newspaper, our customers think we are not giving them good value. • **The computer as appliance.** Volume buying of computers as products in boxes. People think they need our services less.

Table 1.1 SWOT Analysis Table

The diagram above illustrates the nature of a simple SWOT analysis. The important thing to remember is that once the strengths and weaknesses have been identified, a plan needs to be put in place to build on the strengths and to address the weaknesses. That same plan must have the ability to seize the opportunities and eliminate, as much as possible, the threats the business faces.

—

This is the point at which we may welcome back Mama Mboga and the small shop owner. Any form of business, large or medium or small, must have a plan for it to flourish. Larger, more complex organizations will have a more complex SWOT analysis and strategic plan, while smaller operations like the one run by Mama Mboga will have simpler, easier ones. The point to take home is that regardless of the size of a business, it must have a plan. Mama Mboga must know where her business will be five or ten years from now and work tirelessly toward achieving that goal. The shopkeeper must plan five years out and dream of owning something larger—maybe a mall? That is the power of planning. It gives you the ability to think big, to talk big and dream big.

In the next chapter, we shall look at another grossly overlooked aspect of business. It is networking. Among other important issues, you will interact with key ideas in networking like attending events, dressing well and remembering people's names.

Questions

The questions hereunder are designed to review the key discussion points in this chapter. For deeper insights on this topic, readers are encouraged to study the matter broadly.

1. Define strategic planning.
2. Discuss the role of internal and external environment in strategic planning.
3. What is SWOT Analysis?

References

Burnside, B. J. (2002). *The Relationship between the Scope and Formality of Strategic Planning and Organizational Performance*. PhD Thesis, Nova Southeastern University, 2002.

Fleming, P., & Faull, N. (2005). Turning Intentions into Outcomes: A Quick Scorecard to Guide Implementation. *Measuring Business Excellence, 9(3)*, 5-12.

Hopkins, W. E., & Hopkins, S. A. (1997). Strategic Planning-Financial Performance Relationships in Banks: A Causal Examination. *Strategic Management Journal, 18(8)*, 635-652.

Liou, K. T. (2000). Applying Strategic Management to Economic Development: Benefits and challenges. *International Journal of Public Administration, 23(9)*, 1621-1649.

Odundo, E. (2012). *"Environmental Context, Implementation of Strategic Plans and Performance of State Corporations in Kenya"*, Unpublished PhD Thesis, University of Nairobi.

Website: http://en.wikipedia.org/wiki/SWOT_analysis

www.Georgewachiuri.com

http://pas-wordpress-media.s3.amazonaws.com

7 Networking

Networking is one of the most misunderstood concepts in business, yet it is also one of the most important. Indeed, so misunderstood it is that as I carried out my research, I came across a fantastic book titled *Business Networking and Sex,* written by Ivan Misner, the founder and chairman of BNI. Though the title may seem corny and lead you to associate networking with seeking sexual and other relational favors, it actually delves into sound practices in networking. It is the definition drawn from this book that I want us to work with.

Defining Networking

In *Business Networking and Sex*, Ivan Misner defines networking as leveraging your business and personal connections to bring you a regular supply of new business. The concept sounds simple, doesn't it? Don't let that fool you, though. Because it involves relationship building, it can be a deceptively complex process.

He goes on to say:

> Think about it. How many people do you know? How many of these people truly understand what you do? How many of these folks have directed prospects to you as referrals? And how many of those referrals have actually turned into business?

> Business networking is much more than showing up at networking functions, shaking a lot of hands and collecting a bunch of cards. For example, imagine two people attending an event, sizing it up and drawing an imaginary line down the middle. They separate, each taking half the room. At the end of the event, they meet again to see who's collected the most business cards.

> What did they accomplish? They collected a lot of cards that will end up on a shelf, in a drawer, in the trash, or worse yet scanned into a computer so they can spam everyone they just met. Why? What does a business card represent? It's a piece of paper, with ink and images on it. No relationship has been formed. This networking strategy, by itself, isn't an effective use of time, money or energy.

Networking for business growth must be strategic and focused. Not everyone you meet can help move your business forward, but everything you do can be driven by the intention to grow your business. You have total control over whom you meet, where you meet them and how you develop and leverage relationships for mutual benefit.

Networking your business means you have to be proactive. The core of networking is doing something specific each week that is focused on networking for business growth. Make a plan, focus and be consistent. When you understand exactly what business networking is and step up to the challenge, you'll find avenues of opportunity that you may have otherwise never discovered, and you will be making an invaluable investment in the steady growth of your business.

Have we started this with a bang or what? I'll tell you something, we needed to because I want Kenyan and African businessmen and women to know the unrivaled significance of networking in business success. In this chapter, we want to discuss in detail the steps one needs to take to network effectively. The first step, as you may well imagine, is to attend events.

Attend Events and Know People

The first time a friend told me to attend as many events as I possibly could to improve on business contacts, I was stunned and treated the counsel as nothing more than the usual jokes of a bombastic entrepreneur who had made it to the top by hanging with the elite. I did not see the connection between attending events and sales. Today, as the CEO of Optiven Ltd, I have become one of the leading champions of this very concept. At all the seminars and events, where I am invited to facilitate, I make sure this concept is discussed with vigor so that those lucky to be present leave with it as a cornerstone in business performance.

The question many ask, when this matter is discussed, is: what do I do if I was born shy? How about if I am an introvert? This is not an idle question; I have interacted with some painfully shy people and know others who are extreme introverts. Their situation, however, is not an excuse for failure to attend events and get to know all the key players in any line of business beneficial to the growth of their business. A serious entrepreneur will clear the calendar to attend seminars, workshops, galas, shows and any other forum that exposes him or her to folks relevant to growth and enhanced performance in his or her business.

At those events, though, use time wisely by assessing those in attendance and evaluating quickly the ones you need to network with and those who may not add much value to your business—not because they are not important, but because they are not in a line of business that intersects with your interests at all. By picking anybody's business card, and by their introduction, you should be able to tell fairly quickly whether your interests match at all or not. And because time is always a factor in these gatherings, move with speed and interact with as many relevant folks as you can.

Learn to Break the Ice

Breaking the ice is the same thing as saying *to begin the talk*. There are people who have that natural ability to break the ice and talk effortlessly as if they have known the tall stranger they have just met for years. Other people, though, lack that gift and have to be deliberate and wise about how they approach that very stranger—to avoid embarrassment and clumsiness.

The first lesson I had to learn when I started attending events was that these were business events, not dating ones. The men and women who grace those events with their presence are business executives eager to impart knowledge; and also start-up business owners desperate to learn new ideas to propel them to the top. Nobody is at the event to look for a life partner. With that in mind, when you get to the floor of such an event, your opening line should be something about business, not about church or politics. Talk about the rousing speech just delivered by a facilitator or any aspect of business already presented in the gathering.

At the end of the day, though, it all boils down to one thing: common sense. My assumption is that for you to have come as far as making it to such an event, you have used and still retain a healthy amount of common sense in you. Use that great gift the Lord gave you to win people over by how you open your conversation with them. Make sure you exude genuine confidence, concern for growth and credibility. Going on that old adage that network is net worth, bring to the floor of any event your charm offensive and let your demeanor, words and candor speak of nothing else but your desire to grow your business into a giant organization.

Don't Blow Own Trumpet

In an earlier chapter, I advised that you need to talk big for people to take you seriously. You have to wonder what the difference is between talking big and blowing one's own trumpet. To talk big is to shape the thoughts of others about your business with the desire to draw in business while to blow your own trumpet is to announce that you have arrived and may not need any help from anybody. It is a put-off!

In the many events I have attended, people are always quick to read each other and we get to know those who are genuine in their desire to learn and those who blow their trumpets to such levels that the sound becomes deafening and irritating.

People already have a pretty good idea about your many successes and failures when you come to an event. They know how large your bank account is because your bankers may be there; they already know what kind of car you drive because your car dealer may be there; they already know where you buy your suits because your designer may be there; and they already know where you do your hair because your beautician may be there. What this means, therefore, is that blowing your own trumpet at an event may cause disconnect between the reality of your circumstances and the castle in the air you are trying frantically to build.

The wiser thing to do is to vigorously engage people by talking big in terms of your vision and how you intend to achieve it. Make people believe you have the passion and capacity to realize your dream with just a little help from them. From what I've seen, many bankers and other business folks like hanging around and working with people they judge to have fire in the belly to succeed at what they set out to do. Be that person who projects hope, not the one who people judge to lack credibility, seriousness and is probably at the event to pass time rather than network.

Dress the Part

The person who coined the phrase *you are addressed the way you dress* was on to something. This is the kind of wise conclusion one arrives at after years of observation. The truth in this cannot be overstated. Indeed, one is addressed the way he or she dresses. What you wear needs to match your professional attitude. If you are an executive, folks will expect a neat suit, a tie and polished shoes. If you are a plumber, people will expect appropriate gear. And if you are a doctor, folks will expect you to show up in a white doctor's gown and a stethoscope on the neck.

At the university, in a communication class, we were sent into Nairobi offices and asked to dress in different ways to test the reaction of those we interacted with in those offices. The results were astounding. The day we went out dressed well, we were received with courtesy and attended to much faster than the day we all dressed down. The treatment got even worse when we showed up dressed shabbily. The point is—dress speaks to the person you are and it is the first statement you make when you meet someone. Let that statement be about your seriousness, not your carelessness.

Does that mean you have to wear expensive suits even if you cannot afford them? Do you have to lock up so much money in the clothing budget just to impress others? Not at all. In one of his widely-read interviews with a leading business monthly in Kenya, one of the nation's top entrepreneurs and philanthropist, Manu Chandaria, stunned readers when he said he has only four suits— that he gives away one whenever he buys a new one. How many suits does a man need, he asks.

Dressing neatly and professionally is not the same thing as dressing expensively. If you can afford expensive attire, by all means purchase it, but if you cannot, cut your coat according to your cloth—pocket size. People will admire and respect you for living within your budget and having no pretenses about yourself. If you are of relatively smaller means, dressing neatly but cheaper will bring you the same respect it brings a man or woman of greater means who dresses neatly, but expensively. It is all about being credible.

Be Persistent in Networking

The word persistent means *never give up*. This is where that passion we discussed in an earlier chapter comes in. The risk of getting discouraged and giving up is much greater if one lacks passion. I can tell you first-hand that not all experiences at these events are pleasant ones; some are nasty and may lead to discouragement and fear. There will be folks there who are rude, snobbish, crude and downright mean. The way to deal with them is to shake off and keep going.

The thing to remember about persistence is that it breaks resistance. If you keep going to these events and talking passionately about your objectives and desires, chances are one of these days someone who has never paid attention at all just might—especially if you call him or her by name. Memorizing names is one of those priceless gifts you must use if you have it. People are always delighted when they feel you've cared enough to know their name.

Then again, there will be those who remain snobbish even after you have made countless efforts to talk to them. Do not let their snobbishness affect the pace and direction of your vision. By the way you handle them, let it be clear that your focus is built on a solid foundation and will not be destroyed by slights. Take away the punch by thanking them for their time and appreciating their willingness to interact with someone like you—who they may consider not worth their time. That is what it means to network.

Always Have your Business Cards

This is the last factor we want to discuss in this chapter. We already discussed and even showed a sample business card earlier. It is advisable to always have that card with you so that as you network, those who need your contact may have it right there and then. Having no business card when it is asked for defines you as not serious and may cost you business.

There are those who complain that folks no longer keep those cards; that too many people just feed them into a shredder and promptly forget who gave it. That may be true, but it is no reason to avoid carrying business cards. Nobody said that each person you gave the card would turn it into a business with you; *you give it just in case*. For many entrepreneurs, that *just in case* has turned into big business when they least expected it.

So, is networking worth the trouble in the prevailing business environment? Is it worth anybody's time? The answer is a resounding yes. I would not be where I am today had it not been for opening myself up to real networking. I have met great entrepreneurs like Manu Chandaria, Vimal Shah, James Mwangi, Chris Kirubi and a host of others because of networking. I am yet to know what other platform is available that would rival networking in the business world.

Questions

The questions hereunder are designed to review the key discussion points in this chapter. For deeper insights on this topic, readers are encouraged to study the matter broadly.

4. Define networking.
5. What does it mean to break the ice?
6. Discuss the importance of networking in business.

References

Misner, I. (2012*). Business Networking and Sex: Not What You Think.* Entrepreneur press; 1st ed. January 10, 2012.

8 Time Management

Time is one of those precious commodities folks here in Africa have mismanaged with reckless abandon. I still recall the day I had an appointment with someone and agreed to meet at 2:00 p.m. I got to the venue at five minutes to two and hoped the gentleman would trot in any time before or just shortly after two. To my utter shock, he did not show up and never bothered to call at all. At around quarter to three I called and he told me he was just moments away. It wasn't until 2:59 p.m. that he hurried into the meeting venue and said it was still 2:00 after all—because it was 2:59, not 3:00!

That kind of attitude about time is despicable and will not work in today's Kenya or Africa. Business being a time-sensitive venture, needs to be run on time and all aspects of it handled in accordance with agreed-upon timelines. In this chapter we want to discuss the key elements of proper time management and stress their importance in business. The first element we have to consider is what you do in the first twelve minutes of waking up. In other words, how does your day start?

The First Twelve Minutes

The first twelve minutes of your twenty-four hour day are the most important twelve minutes you will have on any given day. They will determine how the rest of your day will play out and even set the tempo for either a vibrant or lackluster demeanor on your part. Like an ancient Indian sage, each of us needs to make those first twelve minutes such an integral part of our waking up that when we do not treat them as something sacred, we feel sick—like something is wrong.

In one of the seminars I conducted for youth in Nairobi, a shy girl put her hand up as I was winding up my presentation and said, her voice tremulous, "Sir, does it matter what time I wake up?"

I didn't get her question right, so I asked, "What do you mean?"

She said, "If I woke up at 9:30 a.m., will my first twelve minutes feel the same as someone's who woke up at 5:00 a.m.?"

The girl had a point. I don't remember what my answer was to her question, but I have since reflected on her question. The general answer is yes, the first twelve minutes are the same for anyone, but there is a caveat. They are only the same for someone with a purpose. If you wake up at 5:00 a.m. without a clear sense of direction in your life those twelve minutes will amount to nothing; in fact they may turn out to be the most stressful ones. If, however, your goals are set right and you know what you need to accomplish, those twelve minutes are a blessing and they serve to spur you on. Having a purpose in life is critical to the nature of your first twelve minutes. If anyone doesn't have a purpose yet, that is the point at which to start.

For many folks, those first twelve minutes are spent in ways that are inspiring indeed, but before we look at them, we should look at what the twelve minutes should do for you when they are handled well.

a. **Clear your mind**. As a business man or woman you have competing interests and merciless demands on your time. There will be places you need to go, people you need to meet and even family matters you need to attend to—all in one day. Your first twelve minutes should be spent putting the day into perspective and weighing the demands by their order of importance. By the time you shut the door behind you and hit the road to your work station, it should be clear what your priorities are and how you will handle them.

b. **Renew your sense of purpose**. This is something many folks take for granted, but it is critical to self-actualization. Your first twelve minutes are a time to reflect on your purpose for being in this world and merging those thoughts with your business goals. It is tragic to wake up each day unaware what the Lord put you in this world to accomplish and how He wants you to go about it.

c. **Give you peace of mind**. In business, there is nothing better than a sense that you have a plan to tackle your challenges and that by a given time you will have solved a problem or met a set goal. Reflecting on those challenges and set goals in your first twelve minutes enables you to think them through and formulate a plan to handle them one by one. That is what peace of mind is made of—knowing that there is a way.

d. **Renew your connection with God**. This is one of those things that happen without some folks even thinking about it. When you wake up and think about your purpose in life, set goals and formulate a plan for them, that act gives you peace of mind. That realm where you find peace of mind is the realm where God exists. For Christians, this is something they already know; for others it is something they attribute to their own wisdom and business acumen. It is a manifestation of God's love that He looks over the businesses of all His children, even those who are yet to accept Christ as a personal Savior.

In those first twelve minutes people do different things, but they need to be things that accomplish the goals listed above for your day to get off on the right footing. When I was at Chinga High, in Nyeri County, I used to have a burning desire to escape poverty and make something meaningful of my life. This desire made me wake up each morning and think about life. I used to look at the roof and just think, marvel about the wealth others had and the lack of it on my family's part. What was I going to do to make money? Was God going to reward my reading efforts?

Each day I woke up to reflect on my life. It was that thinking that cleared my mind and led me to make a critical decision for my life: Books Books Books! Today I wake up to jog and think, but it is no longer about escaping poverty; it is about growing Optiven Ltd and driving it to the top. I challenge you to engage in an activity that gives meaning to your life each morning when you wake up. Give it just twelve minutes, will you?

Have a To-Do-List

A To-Do-List is a list of items you consider priority against the limited time you have in a day. There are many folks who wake up in the morning to make this list and yet others who wait till they get to the office to do it. Regardless of when you do it, a To-Do-List is a key tool in organizing your mind around the activities you intend to accomplish. Here is a sample:

Table 1.2 To-Do-List

Unleash Your Full Potential

There are two elements to a To-Do-List:

a. **Activity**. This is the activity you intend to either accomplish yourself or through an agent. As you have seen, the list has a number of lines, which presupposes the fact that it allows room for you to list the activities in accordance with their order of priority. If possible, this list should be adhered to—unless a situation comes up that demands attention ahead of those listed.

b. **Time**. The sample To-Do-List we've seen (above) does not have room for time, but there are many others that do. Where it concerns appointments, meetings and other activities that have to run on a given time, it is crucial to slot in the activity next to the time it will occur.

The point of a To-Do-List is that it is unwise to go about your day jumping from one event to another without a plan. Doing that deprives you the needed ability to handle the most urgent tasks first, then tackling others in a descending order. And like we said earlier, be sure that you make it to your appointments and meetings on time so that you do not delay those with whom you are scheduled to meet. Like yours, their time is important to them, so you do not have a right to keep them waiting and causing them to run late for their next engagements.

Create Time to Meditate

Meditation is a practice in which an individual trains the mind or induces a mode of consciousness, either to realize some benefit or as an end in and of itself. The term refers to a broad variety of practices—much like the term *sports*—that includes techniques designed to promote relaxation, build internal energy or life force and develop compassion, love, patience, generosity and forgiveness. A particularly ambitious form of meditation aims at effortlessly sustained single-pointed (focused) concentration meant to enable its practitioner to enjoy an indestructible sense of well-being while engaging in any life activity (*Wikipedia*).

As a business person, meditation is a practice we need to engage in so we can sharpen our focus on *only what is good for business.* The reason we need focus is: there are too many distractions and tempting deals that may not be good for business. We need to have that ability, the inner sense, to tell what is good from what is not. Meditating gives us that ability and sets us on a path to sharpening our discipline.

When meditating on business, it is good to focus on issues that grow it like vision, goals, strategic objectives and profits. You need to wrap your mind around ideals that when focused on will inspire you to work at them for the betterment of your business growth.

Does this mean we need to mediate in the same manner Buddhist monks do? Buddhist monks involve awareness in their day-to-day activities as a form of mind-training. Should we be in the famous cross-legged posture each day as we think of our businesses? It would be nice, but you don't have to; there are other ways of doing this. Some of the most effective ways are:

- **Sitting in a church pew alone**. In that church, in that temple or in that mosque, you are the only one who knows why you are there and what you have your mind on. By coming to the church, you are making an effort to align your business goals with the will of God for you. This is wisdom!

- **Visiting nature**. In the days of old, prophets like Moses met the Lord in the stillness of nature—in the Midian Desert. The wilderness provided a great ambience for interaction with divinity. Times may have changed, but the principles of eternity never change. If you want a great place to mediate even today, visit a nature preserve like Karura Forest or Resurrection Gardens, in Karen, where the Catholics have put up a magnificent nature garden for reflection.

- **Sitting alone in your office**. This act offers you the opportunity to use the four familiar walls of your office as a backdrop for thinking deeply about the strides, missteps, opportunities and failures of the past. It is probably the only place where you can have an honest assessment of your business journey because the files, books and other tools of trade are there to nudge you on. Create time each day or once a week to meditate!

- **When you wake up**. Those first twelve minutes come into play here. There are folks who don't wake up to pray, but they wake up to meditate. They spend their first twelve minutes thinking deeply about matters of their business and how to make things better. If this is what will work better for you, do it.

In his bestselling book *The Monk Who Sold His Ferrari*, Robin Sharma discusses meditation in confounding detail and suggests that we all need to mediate for the sake of finding inner peace. He says that our inner peace will be reflected on the outside in our actions. As a businessman or woman, your business will only flourish when your meditation leads you to find that elusive inner peace—the kind of peace that makes you take total control of your desires and actions and assures you of victory because you already know what values are more important in life. These are values like peace, stillness and alignment of one's purpose in life with God's plan.

In my business, meditation has worked wonders for me. It has given me great clarity, drawn me closer to God and made me experience inner peace even in moments when I should have felt the bite of failure. Had it not been for mediation, I would have wandered in the wilderness of pain because I would have not known that inner peace is made of deeper values than having a fat bank account.

Read Favorite Books on Leadership

In the last couple of years, a number of great books have been written on various segments of business: strategic planning, starting a business, marketing, closing a deal and others. Some of these books have been written by business theorists and may lack that final tinge of authenticity borne of years of practice. Others, though, have been written by seasoned businessmen and women and offer practical, timely advice.

The lingering downside to these books is the fact that they were penned by Westerners in environments and circumstances quite different from ours. As great as they are, we are many times forced to contextualize their message and fix ourselves in the frame to imagine some of the very uniquely American or French scenarios they discuss.

In recent years, African authors have emerged and are trying to fill the void by writing books sensitive to our cultural and environmental hue. One such book is the one you have in your hand; others are by leaders in the field like Dr. Edward Odundo, whose book on Strategic Planning is one of the best ever penned by an African; Sam Kariuki, whose book on Entrepreneurship is equally commendable.

In this regard, I urge key business leaders in Africa like Chris Kirubi, Aliko Dangote, James Mwangi, Vimal Shah, Manu Chandaria and others to write books chronicling their experiences to encourage young entrepreneurs. This is necessary because many young people, ready to get into business, may come in fearing that these great men they see around have always been great. Their inspiring story of struggles overcome and victories won could encourage young business owners and keep them going just one more day—till they also become great.

Find time in your busy schedule to read!

Unleash Your Full Potential

Exercise

The Mayo Clinic is a nonprofit medical practice and medical research group based in Rochester, Minnesota. It is the first and largest integrated nonprofit medical group practice in the world, employing more than 3,800 physicians and scientists and 50,900 allied health staff. As I carried out my research on exercise, I came across their words of wisdom on this subject. I couldn't resist bringing you these words verbatim—the seven benefits of exercising.

Exercise controls weight

Exercise can help prevent excess weight gain or help maintain weight loss. When you engage in physical activity, you burn calories. The more intense the activity, the more calories you burn. You don't need to set aside large chunks of time for exercise to reap weight-loss benefits. If you can't do an actual workout, get more active throughout the day in simple ways—by taking the stairs instead of the elevator or by revving up your household chores.

Exercise combats health conditions and diseases

Worried about heart disease? Hoping to prevent high blood pressure? No matter what your current weight, being active boosts high-density lipoprotein (HDL), or "good," cholesterol and decreases unhealthy triglycerides. This one-two punch keeps your blood flowing smoothly, which decreases your risk of cardiovascular diseases. In fact, regular physical activity can help you prevent or manage a wide range of health problems and concerns, including stroke, metabolic syndrome, type 2 diabetes, depression, certain types of cancer, arthritis and falls.

Exercise improves mood

Need an emotional lift? Or need to blow off some steam after a stressful day? A workout at the gym or a brisk 30-minute walk can help. Physical activity stimulates various brain chemicals that may leave you feeling happier and more relaxed. You may also feel better about your appearance and yourself when you exercise regularly, which can boost your confidence and improve your self-esteem.

Exercise boosts energy

Winded by grocery shopping or household chores? Regular physical activity can improve your muscle strength and boost your endurance. Exercise and physical activity deliver oxygen and nutrients to your tissues and help your cardiovascular system work more efficiently. And when your heart and lungs work more efficiently, you have more energy to go about your daily chores.

Exercise promotes better sleep

Struggling to fall asleep or to stay asleep? Regular physical activity can help you fall asleep faster and deepen your sleep. Just don't exercise too close to bedtime, or you may be too energized to fall asleep.

Exercise puts the spark back into your sex life

Do you feel too tired or too out of shape to enjoy physical intimacy? Regular physical activity can leave you feeling energized and looking better, which may have a positive effect on your sex life. But there's more to it than that. Regular physical activity can lead to enhanced arousal for women. And men who exercise regularly are less likely to have problems with erectile dysfunction than are men who don't exercise.

Exercise can be fun

Exercise and physical activity can be a fun way to spend some time. It gives you a chance to unwind, enjoy the outdoors or simply engage in activities that make you happy. Physical activity can also help you connect with family or friends in a fun social setting. So, take a dance class, hit the hiking trails or join a soccer team. Find a physical activity you enjoy, and just do it. If you get bored, try something new.

The bottom line on exercise

As a businessman or woman, one who intends to remain robust, exercise and physical activity are a great way to feel better, gain health benefits and have fun. Aim for at least thirty minutes of physical activity every day. Don't allow yourself to be like the men and women who pack weight and watch helplessly as their health deteriorates, business suffers and life becomes meaningless. There is always something you can do to keep fit and live a healthy lifestyle. Our friends at Mayo Clinic have told us the benefits. It is upon us to heed their advice.

Prayer

The late American singer Jake Hess popularized the song *Prayer Unlocks the Door* when he sung with the Gaither Homecoming team. Many business folks have failed to make a connection between prayer and profits. Prayer is indeed the key to heaven and it unlocks the doors. I know a businesswoman who believed so firmly in prayer that whenever business was down, she went to a secluded place to fast. One day I caught up with her going to the Resurrection Gardens to pray. When I asked whether it worked, she nodded and told me to try it.

I tried and today I know that prayer is key to business. I spend time praying and thanking God for the blessings of wealth, which He has put in my hands to manage. I am keenly aware that one day He will ask me to give an account of how I handled that wealth. On that day, I will want to look Him in the eye and say I fed the orphans, clothed the widows, put a roof over the destitute and built churches in the land. If your business does not keep you on your knees in daily prayer, you haven't made the connection between business and God yet.

Questions

The questions hereunder are designed to review the key discussion points in this chapter. For deeper insights on this topic, readers are encouraged to study the matter broadly.

1. What is the significance of the first twelve minutes in time management?
2. Discuss the role of a To-Do-List.
3. What role does exercise play in time management?

References

Sharma, R. (2009). *The Monk Who Sold His Ferrari: A Spiritual Fable about Fulfilling Your Dreams and Reaching Your Destiny.* Harper Element.

Website: en.wikipedia.org/wiki/Meditation

www.mayoclinic.org/healthy-living/fitness/in.../exercise/art

9 Motivation

Motivation is a theoretical construct used to explain behavior. It is the scientific word used to represent the reasons for our actions, for our desires, for our needs, etc. Motives are hypothetical constructs used to explain why people do what they do. A motive is what prompts a person to act in a certain way or at least to develop a visible inclination for specific behavior. For example, when someone eats food to satisfy the need of hunger, or when a student does his work diligently in school because he wants a good grade. Both show a similar connection between what we do and why we do it (*Wikipedia*).

The question we have to grapple with in this chapter is: what motivates an entrepreneur? This is one of the most important elements in business and we have to discuss it with the seriousness it deserves. To get an answer about what motivates entrepreneurs, I had to look at the life of folks like Warren Buffet, Richard Branson and Bill Gates abroad; and Manu Chandaria, Vimal Shah and James Mwangi here in Kenya. There is a common thread that weaves the fabric of their experiences: motivation.

The rise of Bill Gates, much like the rise of Chandaria and Mwangi, is written on a template of trials, failures and triumphs. For these giant entrepreneurs of the waning years of the twentieth century and opening years of the twenty first century, there was never a dull moment in their rise. Their life was colored with painful encounters, moments of distress and discouragement and days of great agonizing. Because they overcame those early distresses and triumphed over such adversities, we are wise to borrow from their vast experiences by reading stories about their lives. In this narrative, however, we want to focus on how motivation affects business.

Passion

In an earlier chapter, we discussed passion as a critical element in business because it is what gives you the energy to keep rolling when you would much rather fold up and call it quits. It is because of the centrality of passion that it is advisable to start a business along the lines of something that fires you up when you think about it.

In the case of Bill Gates, he fell in love with an old computer at school and got so fascinated by its ability to churn out patterns that he later found no other calling in life but to understand the computer better. Here is an account of how that love affair started—in *Wikipedia*:

> At thirteen, Bill Gates enrolled in the Lakeside School, an exclusive preparatory school. When he was in the eighth grade, the Mothers Club at the school used the meagre proceeds from Lakeside School's rummage sale to buy a Teletype Model 33 ASR terminal and a block of computer time on a General Electric (GE) computer for the school's students. Gates took an interest in programming the GE system in BASIC, and was excused from math classes to pursue his interest. He wrote his first computer program on this machine: an implementation of tic-tac-toe that allowed users to play games against the computer. Gates was fascinated by the machine and how it would always execute software code perfectly. When he reflected back on that moment, he said, "There was just something neat about the machine."

From that humble beginning, Gates never looked back. He saw each challenge and trial, and there were many that came his way, as just one more adversary to be overcome. He faced banning in school for introducing bugs into a system and later dropped out from Harvard, when he felt there was much more to be discovered out of class than in it—at least in so far as concerned computers.

It was the passion to discover greater things, to reach for new horizons, that kept Gates going and should keep each of us in business. Give meaning to what you do and make it a thing of fascination. In Optiven Ltd, for example, I keep asking myself what kind of Africa we would have if we got each African into a great house? Would we be like America or would we be even better? For me, that is a passion thing, it fascinates me, it gives me the motivation to wake up each morning and fires me up to think of innovative ways to make my dream of good housing for Africa a reality in this century.

Keep Energy High

The energy you bring, on a daily basis, to your business is a good indicator of whether you are passionate about what you do or not. Once you have identified what you feel the Lord called you in this world to accomplish, channel all your energies in scaling the wall toward the peak each day and every moment of your waking hours. The life story of Warren Buffet is illustrative of this thought. From selling chewing gum and Coca Cola door-to-door to selling newspapers; and later being rejected at Harvard Business School, what you see is a man who had to keep his energy high and stay focused on his dream. Here is a glimpse from *Wikipedia*:

> As a child, Buffett displayed an interest in making and saving money. He sold chewing gum, Coca-Cola and at times weekly magazines door to door. He worked in his grandfather's grocery store. While still in his high school, he made money delivering newspapers, selling golf balls and stamps and detailing cars, among other means. On his first income tax return in 1944, Buffett took a $35 deduction for the use of his bicycle and watch on his paper route. In 1945, as a high school sophomore, Buffett and a friend spent $25 to purchase a used pinball machine, which they placed in the local barber shop. Within months, they owned several machines in different barber shops.
>
> Buffett's interest in the stock market and in investing dated to schoolboy days he spent in the customers' lounge of a stock brokerage near his father's own brokerage office. On a trip to New York City at age ten, he made a point to visit

the New York Stock Exchange. At 11, he bought three shares of Cities Service Preferred for himself, and three for his sister. In high school, he invested in a business owned by his father and bought a farm worked by a tenant farmer.

In 1947 Buffett entered the Wharton School of the University of Pennsylvania. He studied there for two years and even joined the Alpha Sigma Phi fraternity. He later transferred to the home-state University of Nebraska, Lincoln, where at only nineteen he graduated with a Bachelor of Science in business administration.

He later applied for his masters at the Harvard Business School, but was rejected. Disappointed, he enrolled at the Columbia Business School after learning that Benjamin Graham, author of *The Intelligent Investor*, a Buffett favorite, and David Dodd, two well-known securities analysts, taught there. Buffet earned his Master of Science in economics from Columbia in 1951 and he later attended the New York Institute of Finance.

The stories of these great businessmen are not slotted in this book for fun; they are here to instill in us the value of keeping us focused on our vision. Warren Buffet, much like Bill Gates, opened himself up to be guided by three critical factors:

a. Vision,
b. Fascination, and
c. Focus (energy level).

When these three core factors are brought together in an entrepreneur and packaged into values, motivation is the end result; and where there is motivation, there can be no quitting because winners don't quit!

Managing Failure

It is true that winners don't quit, but it is also true that they experience some of the most discouraging failures. The first lesson to learn about failure is that just because you failed doesn't mean you are a failure; you need to dust up and keep going. Manu Chandaria is one of those who dusted up after the depression of the 1930s and kept going. Described today as one of Kenya's leading industrialists and awarded the Elder of the Burning Spear (EBS), one of Kenya's top awards for a civilian, he faced failure many times, but he always treated each failure as something to learn from.

Shortly before Chandaria and his brother's return to Kenya, their family had amassed substantial holdings that made it possible for their entry into the steel and aluminum industry. Chandaria's future father-in-law had organized a group of ten individuals to acquire saucepan manufacturer Kenya Aluminum, an enterprise that had folded during the depression, from an Indian merchant in 1929, although this group eventually broke up to pursue different ventures some twenty years later. Such were the earnest beginnings of the future $2.5 billion Comcraft Group. With the onset of the 1950s and 1960s came the expansion of Comcraft to other African countries such as Ethiopia, Nigeria, Congo, India, and Zambia, with Chandaria being charged with business affairs in Uganda and Congo. He is today the chairman of Comcraft Group and the Bank of India Advisory Committee in Nairobi among others. His personal business interests are extensive and span the vast of the Kenyan economy and as well as 50 other countries (*Wikipedia*).

What would have become of Manu Chandaria had he looked at the collapse of his family's business during the depression and decided he didn't want to burn his fingers like his parents had? Instead of getting cold with fear, he looked at that failure as a stepping stone to something greater—because he was *willing* and ready *to learn* from it. He studied the structure of that business and noted why it couldn't withstand the winds of a

Unleash Your Full Potential

depression, then set out to build a foundation firm enough for his future ventures. In other words, he was ready for correction.

Take Correction Kindly

Correction is not one of the easiest meals to take even when it is served on a king's table. It is hard because the meal comes marinated with the bitter herbs of failure and fear. The amazing rise of James Mwangi as a leading innovator in Kenya is riddled with moments when he had to be corrected by no other than a widowed, peasant mother in the chilling Aberdares area, in Kenya. In his biography, *James Mwangi: A Life Stranger than Fiction*, you get a glimpse of how he dealt with correction as a child—something he kept as a virtue all his life:

> There was no time for childish games – everyone had to pitch in to keep the home fires burning. James, like the rest of his siblings, had to put in his share of chores – tending to the livestock, making charcoal, selling fruits and other produce for small margins.
>
> Although the family was poor, "my mother ensured that we were disciplined and she laid out a set of values which became anchors in our lives," Mwangi recalls. "There was one point on

which she was not prepared to back down or compromise one iota – that was education. She decided that her children, all her children, would be educated – no matter what it took," Mwangi said.

As Mwangi talked, a picture of the mother, Grace Wairimu, began to emerge. Here was a woman, well past the first flush of youth, who was straining every sinew and using all her ingenuity not only to feed and clothe her children, but was adamant that they not only go to school but learn. When she insisted that her daughters also attend school, a shudder of apprehension went through the village of Kangema, their home. Girls did not go to school. There was a lot of shaking of heads, but Grace Wairimu was adamant. Perhaps this inured the young James Mwangi to criticism and allowed him to ignore a lot of head shaking later in life when he was trying to breathe life in a defunct organization.

Despite enormous social and financial problems, Grace Wairimu ensured that all her children were educated. "Much later," Mwangi remembers, "when I had my own four sons, their granny supervised their education and kept them away

Unleash Your Full Potential

from harmful teenage activities going around. When they got their school reports, they first went to their granny, rather than me, their father. She passed on a wealth of wisdom through storytelling and, in many ways, molded my family."

Correction is critical to motivation. It is a virtue that is best learnt when one is young, like James Mwangi did, but if not learnt then, must be learnt as one gets into business. There will be many issues and circumstances you have never encountered before and for which you need to be advised and corrected. If you allow yourself room to learn and be corrected, your business will grow, but if you insist on doing things your way, your business will go with you that way—right into oblivion!

—

Role Model

A role model is a person you admire from afar and inspires you by the way he or she handles the various situations of life. To be motivated, especially in business, we all need to have a role model, someone we look up to and aspire to be like. For me, that person is James Mwangi. I admire his great work ethic, his demeanor, his courage under fire and his belief in the use of wealth to transform the lives of others.

You don't have to be close friends with role models to learn from them; all you have to do is watch them. I recall my fascination with James Mwangi the first time I met him. I didn't want to overstep my bounds because I was just one among those who were in attendance at the conference, but I made it a point to tell him he was my role model. I watched as his face beamed with a smile and knew that he appreciated my sincerity.

Having a role model builds on your passion and keeps you motivated in your business. The man or woman who is your model keeps your mind preoccupied with ideas about becoming like him or her. You strive to be a better businessman or woman—and even a better person—because of your desire is to follow in your role model's footsteps. You want to be like Mwangi!

Mentor

A mentor is a person you talk to and can tell you the truth without shame. It is that mentor who can advise, correct and scold you when need arises. My mentor is Vimal Shah, the Chairman of the BIDCO Group. Having been in corporate circles in Kenya over the years, he knows the ins and outs of the business terrain in Kenya—and even much of Africa and the world.

As you get deeper into business, you will need to tie yourself to a mentor and let the person know you regard him or her as such. This is the person that will tell you the truth regardless of circumstances and will offer you invaluable counsel on the best course of action. He or she is the person who will give you workable ideas and send you out of your private talks motivated because the future looks bright after the candid talk. If you have never had a mentor, the time to think seriously about one is now. Allow yourself the space to be guided by a voice of reason—one you can trust in good and in bad times. That is what being mentored is all about.

Questions

The questions hereunder are designed to review the key discussion points in this chapter. For deeper insights on this topic, readers are encouraged to study the matter broadly.

1. Discuss the role of motivation in business performance.
2. Why is it important to take correction kindly?
3. Who is:
   a. A mentor?
   b. A role model?

References

Websites: africanbusinessmagazine.com/.../james-mwangi-a-life-
stranger-than-fiction

en.wikipedia.org/wiki/Bill_Gates

en.wikipedia.org/wiki/Manu_Chandaria

en.wikipedia.org/wiki/Motivation

10 Innovation

In my past seminars, this was one of the few subjects I approached with a degree of hesitation because it happened to be the one area I felt least prepared to handle effectively. The challenge was that I felt Africa offered limited space for great innovation and talking about it could only make me look like a dreamer. Most references to great innovators of our time inevitably centered on regions of the world far removed from ours and even those regions, if not in the Western world, only nurtured those lucky innovators courtesy of Western organizations like the World Bank, the IMF or a Western nation that spotted and nurtured that potential.

For us to have a clear understanding of what innovation is, we need to begin by defining it. I have seen those who have defined innovation as imagination, common sense and other ideas of that nature, but those definitions are misleading and may actually harm innovativeness as a solid rock upon which African businesses need to be anchored. In this chapter, we want to look at what this rock is and how it can be used to build businesses in the twenty-first century Africa. The fact that there have been few innovators in Kenya and around Africa cannot deter us from creating them in this brave new century, which many prognosticators have projected to be the century for Africa's rise. So what is innovation?

Defining Innovation

Innovation can be viewed as the application of better solutions that meet new requirements, unarticulated needs, or existing market needs. This is accomplished through more effective products, processes, services and technologies, or through ideas that are readily available to markets, to governments and society in general. The term innovation can be defined as something original and, as a consequence, new, that "breaks into" the market or society. While a novel (great) device is often described as an innovation, in economics, management science and other fields of practice and analysis, innovation is generally considered to be a process that brings together various novel ideas in a way that they have an impact on society (*Wikipedia*).

In this definition, the line that should stand out is: *in a way that they have an impact on society*. In Kenya, one of the greatest innovators of our time is James Mwangi. The jovial man is credited with turning a hitherto unknown financial institution, Equity Bank, into Kenya's bank of choice for the "small" man. At the height of its operations, it was rumored that the bank developed such innovative ideas to lending that it even accepted cows as collateral. It also opened its doors earlier than other more established banks and gave loans to folks elitist banks would never touch. It was a revolutionary approach the likes of which Kenyans had never seen.

It didn't take long before banks across Kenya felt the heat of Equity's innovative fire and started to relax their lending requirements—and even opening and closing hours. What James Mwangi achieved was to turn Equity Bank into a force for good. As a banking institution, no other lender has so dramatically lifted millions of Kenyans out of poverty like this bank has. Because of it, many people came to believe in themselves and many businesses were started in the nation.

Mwangi's approach is a classic example of give a man fish, he will ask for another tomorrow; give him a net and he will catch his own fish. This is the essence of innovation. The idea is to look for ways of finding those nets in such large numbers that when more men have them, the impact is felt in society.

This approach is different from philanthropy, where an individual or a company has dedicated some of its huge profits to giving back to society. Whereas philanthropy is great and has been recognized world over as worthy, it is far better to create institutions and systems that enable people to fish for themselves. A man or woman who has made billions of shillings, for example, should make funds available to build a school, a training center or start a lending institution where people can borrow money to change the direction of their lives through business.

Avoid Copying Others

In an earlier chapter, we talked about the place of role models and mentors; we have also discussed business models that we would like to borrow from. The question we need to answer, therefore, is: is there a difference between borrowing ideas and copying others?

To answer this question, let us look at what it takes to be truly innovative:

> In the organizational context, innovation may be
> linked or tied to positive changes in efficiency, in

productivity, in quality, in competitiveness, and in market share (*Wikipedia*).

The words employed in this descriptive sentence are all measurable. You can measure efficiency, productivity, quality and competitiveness in output. There is no way one can copy these; and it may actually be harmful to try to replicate the successes of another firm in your own firm. It is far wiser to deliberately think things through and be innovative. Copying others is a way of declaring that you refuse to think, to be innovative.

Innovation, in a fast-paced business environment like the world offers today, involves the use of technology to spur growth. Businessmen and women who boldly avail to themselves opportunities like the use of programs and systems designed to streamline service delivery are the ones who will taste the greatness of business in this brave new world. There is no place for men and women who will shun technology in running a business today. And the point is—no one can copy another person's interaction with technology; each of us must learn how to integrate these modern ways of trading into our businesses for systems to spur growth and efficiency.

At Optiven Ltd, we have gone out of our way to introduce modern technology into our business. We use modern real estate systems and analogies to craft the best solutions for our customers. Our value added plots are an innovative approach to selling land already upgraded and in compliance with our policy of placing families in modern homes in a great environment.

Our head office, at Barclays Plaza, in Nairobi's CBD, are also an innovative approach to real estate management. We took the bold step to get into the big office at a time most start-up real estate firms were reluctant to engage much money in renting such facilities. We judged, correctly, that for customers to take us seriously, we had to locate our operations in a place that reflected our core values and spoke to our mission.

Today we look back and are delighted by that innovative approach to confidence-building in our customers. We have been rewarded and have two trophies in our office to show for it. One of those trophies was given on a night we least expected to win it. When it was all done, we sat there astounded to have been placed top among Kenya's SMEs. The market had rewarded our innovativeness!

We have since learnt that a number of competing real estate companies are trying to copy Optiven Ltd's path to success, but they miss the point. It is not about copying, but borrowing. They can borrow our ideas and

Unleash Your Full Potential

even improve them to realize better performance and greater output, but they cannot copy what we have done because the systems and approaches that have worked for us are based on our core values and our vision—not theirs.

Be Original

Being original is at the core of being innovative. It is a call to be creative. Another great innovator of our time is the Bangladeshi social entrepreneur, who much like our own James Mwangi, developed innovative ways to lend money to people traditional banks had left behind. He formulated ways of bringing the poor into his society's mainstream by extending loan facilities to them. For his innovativeness and originality in thinking, he has been rewarded by an appreciative nation and an inspired global community. A description of his prowess reads as follows in *Wikipedia:*

> Muhammad Yunus (Bengali: মুহাম্মদ ইউনূস, born on the 28th of June 1940), is a Bangladeshi social entrepreneur, banker, economist and civil society leader who was awarded the prestigious Nobel Peace Prize for founding the Grameen Bank and pioneering the twin concepts of microcredit and microfinance. These tailored loans are given to

entrepreneurs too poor to qualify for traditional bank loans. In 2006, Yunus and the Grameen Bank were jointly awarded the Nobel Peace Prize "for their efforts through microcredit to create economic and social development from below." The Norwegian Nobel Committee noted that "lasting peace cannot be achieved unless large population groups find ways in which to break out of poverty" and that "across cultures and civilizations, Yunus and Grameen Bank have shown that even the poorest of the poor can work to bring about their own development." Yunus has since received several other national and international honors. He received the United States Presidential Medal of Freedom in 2009 and the Congressional Gold Medal in 2010.

That is what originality means to me. It is looking at the circumstances around you and believing there is a silver lining in the prevailing desperation. That silver lining can only be seen and turned into a blessing if someone uses elements provided by the desperation to harness them for the greater good of society. No business will ever grow where creativity and originality lack.

Don't Fight Competitors in Public

Where else would you fight them if not in court, one student asked me when I made the statement. Of course there are moments you will be drawn into a public spat through court summons and media attacks, but by and large it is wise to avoid public spats with competition especially if the company drawing you in is one that stands to gain much more from that publicity than your company. It may well be that the publicity they enjoy out of your tribulations is what drives them rather than anything morally or legally substantive.

In the event that a public spat is a necessity, be sure to turn that publicity to your advantage by projecting your company as a paragon of virtue. Demonstrate that your company is keen to play by the rules and is even more eager to uplift the community by its presence. Nothing works better for a company than a positive image, especially one built over a long period of time. An attack on a company with a long track record of virtue can only serve to strengthen it and not harm it.

Team Building

This is the final segment in this chapter on innovation. It would be unwise to end the chapter without discussing team building because this is one of the ways innovation is encouraged and nursed. A company that wishes to be successful must build strong teams that will take the lead in generating creative ideas for trading.

In business, we may describe a team as a group of people selected to look into an aspect of operations. The team, once constituted, should be under capable leadership and should be responsible for advising management on creative ways to move the agenda of the company forward. When all constituted teams work in harmony in a company, the company experiences what thought-leaders in management call homeostasis.

The teams one builds should be molded to reflect the core values of the company and revel in the company's vision. This is because innovation is not always a fun thing to do, and may even be harder where systems are imbalanced because of varying degrees of strength in individual teams. The diagram on next page illustrates the core impediments to homeostasis:

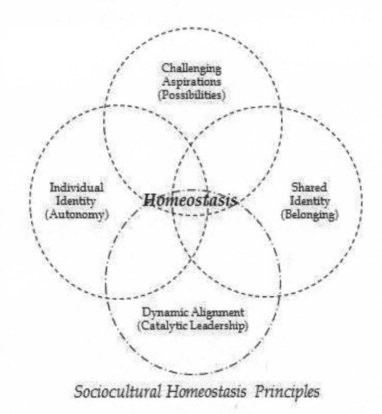

Sociocultural Homeostasis Principles

Figure 1.3 Sociocultural Homeostasis Principles

The same dynamics that apply in a sociocultural setting are the ones that apply in a company. For there to be calm (homeostasis) in a company, there must be teams capable of the task of formulating ideas, which lead to overcoming challenges, providing solutions and keeping the company always one step ahead of the innovative curve of competitors.

And finally, when a team works well and achieves great results for the company, it is always wise to reward it. In some of the books on leadership I have read, this is one of the areas in which companies fail their employees. In fact, I came across many examples of companies that don't even have a reward policy. Such companies enjoy the innovative ideas of teams within it, but slap them in the cheek by failing to reward performance. What failure to reward performance says is this: *we don't give a damn about what you do for us; if you wish you can ship out!*

I'm sure James Mwangi and Muhammad Yunus and Bill Gates rewarded teams that excelled in innovation and created the amazing systems the world has cherished over the years. At Optiven Ltd we have followed in the footsteps of these great business leaders and crafted a rewards policy for our employees. It is ethical, human and respectful to reward excellence; failure to reward excellence will always lead to nonperformance.

Questions

The questions hereunder are designed to review the key discussion points in this chapter. For deeper insights on this topic, readers are encouraged to study the matter broadly.

1. Define innovation.
2. What is the role of originality in innovation?
3. Discuss the concept of homeostasis in innovation.

References

Website: en.wikipedia.org/wiki/Innovation

http://en.wikipedia.org/wiki/Muhammad_Yunus

http://www.unmanagement.com/wp-content/uploads/2013/06/Catalytic-Leadership-and-Sociocultural-Homeostasis-2.pdf

11 Governance

Governance is the final chapter in this book. You may be tempted to wonder why we didn't start with it and you are right to ask. The answer is this—just about everything we have discussed in this book relates to governance in one way or another. When we talk about governance at this level, however, we bump up the scale of discussion to a whole new altitude. In this chapter, we are going to deal with issues like cash flow, projections, discipline and hiring of staff. This is the point at which everything we have discussed harmonizes and comes together in what is known collectively as governing.

Defining Governance

Governance refers to "all the processes of governing, whether undertaken by a government, a market or a network, whether over a family, tribe, formal or informal organization or territory and whether through laws, norms, power or language." It relates to "the processes of interaction and decision-making among the actors involved in a collective problem that lead to the creation, reinforcement, or reproduction of social norms and institutions" (*Wikipedia*).

In the just-concluded chapter we talked in detail about innovation and teams and how individual teams in a company come together to form a cohesive whole. For that cohesive whole to emerge, there has to be a proper governing structure that harmonizes thought, findings and goals and makes all teams and all the levels of management work toward a shared vision.

Since we have already discussed managerial hierarchy and organograms in another chapter, we need to focus on other matters related to governance like cash flow.

Cash Flow

Cash flow is the movement of money into or out of a business, project, or financial product. It is usually measured during a specified, limited period of time. Measurement of cash flow can be used for calculating other parameters that give information on a company's value and situation (*Wikipedia*).

There are many people in business who have no idea how critical to their survival cash flow is. This may affect smaller businesses more acutely, but it affects larger operations as well. Thought-leaders in business have all kinds of learned ways of describing this phenomenon, but what it boils down to is this: that you need to release money in a manner that is commensurate with how fast money comes in. It does not make sense to spend money at a rate far faster than the rate at which it comes back to the company. There have to be policies and systems that are used to govern the flow of cash into and out of a business. The table below illustrates this point:

Description	Amount ($)	totals ($)
Cash flow from operations		**+10**
Sales (paid in cash)	+30	
Materials	-10	
Labor	-10	
Cash flow from financing		**+40**
Incoming loan	+50	
Loan repayment	-5	
Taxes	-5	
Cash flow from investments		**-10**
Purchased capital	-10	
Total		**+40**

Table 1.3 Cash flow

Projections

Another area of governance critical to performance is projection and budgeting. You cannot budget until you have projected how you expect your sales to behave over a period of time. That projection is based on how past sales and overall business systems behaved over a similar period of time in the past business calendar and how you realistically assess them to follow that same pattern, barring an unforeseen departure from the contemplated norm.

To project credibly, there are a couple of elements that one needs to bring into account:

a.   **The environment**. If the prevailing environment has remained the same over the past set period of assessment as it is today, one can safely project that sales and earnings will behave the same.

b.   **Demographics**. The unpredictable shifting nature of demographics is something companies watch keenly because it determines how sales turn out. Based on how those shifts take place, one can reasonably project earnings—either to go higher or to drop.

c.   **Leadership**. This is one of the key pillars in the projection of future earnings. If the leaders of a company who spurred growth remain in place, it is reasonable to project similar growth and earnings over a comparable period of time, but if changes are made in leadership, it is wiser to adopt a wait and see attitude and make only modest projections.

Budgets

It is based on those calendar projections, which we have discussed above, that budgets are made. In complex companies, budgets are usually made to cover key items like employee salaries, product advertising, recurrent expenditure, entertainment, continuing education and other relevant needs. In smaller operations, however, budgets cover fewer items and are based on more modest projections. In my research, I came across a website called *AllBusiness*. Here is what it says about projections and budgeting:

> Your budget will assist you when tracking the flow and progress of your business by providing you with a picture of how much you are spending and in which areas you are exceeding your projected spending limits. A budget can be prepared for a specific area such as promotion and marketing or a special project or as an overall guideline for your small business.

Unleash Your Full Potential

To formulate your budget, you will come up with a reasonable projection of your sales. The budget will set forth the cash available to the business. For a new business you will include the funding you have obtained through personal financing, loans, investments, selling shares of stock and other sources. Once you have a realistic forecast of the money you anticipate having available, you can look at the potential categories of expenses and determine a realistic amount to spend in each category. Most budgets are usually works in progress with several revisions.

Once projections and budgets are done and all the other issues we have discussed in previous chapters are well addressed, a business is finally ready to run well. Its running well, however, will depend on the kind of staff you hire to steer the ship. This is why I want us to close this book by discussing a human resource issue.

Hiring and Firing

A chapter on governance cannot be concluded without a rigorous discussion on hiring and firing of employees. This is one of the most difficult things to do. Indeed, in nations like the United States, managers and co-workers have been killed by their colleagues whose services have been terminated. We should begin by agreeing on a basic fact here—that firing a worker should be done as a final resort, not arbitrarily and in a huff.

The people you hire should be brought in because they have passed an interview that evaluates the core skills they bring to the company and not because of any other considerations. Among the issues to be considered are:

a. **The right attitude**. A company runs on the basis of its vision, its mission and core values and every employee must have an attitude that fits in well with these orientations.

b. **Passion for role**. An employee who has the right attitude will quite likely have the right passion for his or her role in the company. If one were to be brought in as an accountant, he must have a passion for accounting for every last cent; and if one were brought in as a manager, she must have a passion for the vision of the company.

c. **Requisite skills**. This is where many companies have gone wrong. They hire people on the basis of nepotism, religion and other considerations against the interests of business. Each employee should be hired strictly on the basis of the skills they bring to the role they are expected to play. An accountant should not be asked to be a public relations manager and a janitor should not be asked to be a financial controller.

Hiring is generally done by faith because the CV and that great referral a prospective employee slaps on the table during an interview could be nothing but exaggerated claims. This is why once staff are hired you need to formulate ways of motivating them, training them and even giving them a coach to work with them. It is only after you have gone this extra mile in meeting their adjustment needs that you can later fire them if they don't live up to expectations.

Because of the trauma of firing, however, it is advisable to avoid hiring people you cannot fire. Do not put people on your payroll that when things go wrong you will be forced to look the other way. Relatives and friends fit the bill and should be brought in only after they have signed a pledge to act within the framework of the company's code of conduct or they will be forced to resign—not fired—but forced to resign.

Questions

The questions hereunder are designed to review the key discussion points in this chapter. For deeper insights on this topic, readers are encouraged to study the matter broadly.

1. Discuss the role of a manager in an organization.
2. What is cash flow and how does it affect budgeting in a business?
3. Why is it important to have a sound policy for hiring and firing in an organization?

References

Website: www.allbusiness.com/accounting-reporting/budget-Budget

en.wikipedia.org/wiki/Cash_flow

12 Conclusion

In this book I have discussed all the elements of business I needed to discuss. The issues raised here are among those I have presented before Kenya's young people at various forums. Because of their depth, I needed to lay them within the pages of a book and present them in this coherent format for any reader with a desire to begin a business to benefit from my experiences.

If I were a storyteller, this is the point at which I would be expected to say: and they lived happily ever after. Since this is a book on starting and running a business, however, I will say this: and they went out to put into practice all the lessons they had learnt.

The future of business in Africa is promising and is getting even better by the day. The many challenges we faced, most of them related to political instability, have been sorted out or are being sorted out now in many nations. The economic blocs like ECOWAS, EAC and IGAD are also doing their part to create huge markets for homegrown products. In this new scheme of things, those of us who see the future through the eyes of a sage will take advantage of the great environment.

It is my hope that we will all accept the challenge to graduate from our universities and start businesses rather than toil in the alleys of hopelessness looking for jobs that are not there. As educated young people, you and I are the future of Africa. This continent will only rise to a key player in global business if we start companies that will compete those elsewhere.

The Kenyan government, under the engaged leadership of presidents Mwai Kibaki and Uhuru Kenyatta, has taken the lead in formulating policies favorable to local and global investment. It is now upon each of us to answer the call of our time: wealth creation for a better life for all. Will you be counted when the roll is called?

Index

www.optiven.co.ke

www.optivenfoundation.org

www.mountaingates.com

www.OptiCareInsurance.com

Optiven Limited is a Real Estate company founded to empower property investors in Africa. We are in the Business of settling Kenyans. Optiven is the market leader in the industry and was crowned Number One Company in Kenya and the Best in Real Estate Under Top 100 Mid- Size Company Awards 2014/15

Optiven Foundation concentrates on making the world a better place through offering essential services to humanity. Our main focus is the provision of quality education opportunities to millions of needy children across Africa, poverty alleviation, promotion of health and environmental protection.

Mountain Gates is a construction company and a subsidiary of Optiven Group of Companies. Our main focus is the provision of cost-effective housing across Eastern Africa. The company aspires to provide home solutions through the most efficient and effective techniques. The company thrives on professionalism, honesty, customer-focus and innovation.

OptiCare Insurance Brokers focuses on the provision of premier insurance brokerage services to insured clients. It is customer focused, accountable and reliable with a touch of empathy. OptiCare Insurance Brokers is the preferred Insurance brokerage company of choice. We aim to meet and exceed customer expectations.

Other Great Books By
Sahel Publishing Association

1. *Judy's World*, by Dr. Nicholas Letting
2. *Listen Little Children*, by Lillian Omuga
3. *Remember*, by Dr. Vincent Orinda
4. *Walking On The Edge,* by Joe Muchekehu
5. *The Guy Who Fired His Boss*, by Sam Kariuki
6. *Understanding Arthritis*, by Dr. Omondi Oyoo
7. *The Dance Party,* by K.B. Onyango
8. *The Doctrine Of Strategic Planning,* by Dr. Edward Odundo
9. *Heal Our Land,* by Sam Okello
10. *Raising A Healthy Child,* by Petronila Muthoni Agwata
11. *Soaring Like An Eagle,* by George Wachiuri
12. *Luo Kitgi Gi Timbegi E Ngima Masani,* by PLO Lumumba

There will be many more books that will answer life's toughest questions for you, because as we always say, Sahel Publishing Association's promise is: Books That Speak To Your Hopes and Fears. Call us today**: 0715.596.106 or 0731.651.927**. Talk to one of Africa's most-sought ghostwriters and editors, Hon Sam Okello, about your writing dreams!

Visit any of our authors at: www.amazon.com
Our website: www.sahelpublishing.net
We are in Kenya, the U.S.A., The U.K. and India
Publish your book with us today!

Made in the USA
Las Vegas, NV
19 November 2021